The History of the parish of Kington St. Michael, County of Wilts.

John Edward Jackson

The BiblioLife Network

GUIDE TO FOLD-OUTS, MAPS and OVERSIZED IMAGES

In an online database, page images do not need to conform to the size restrictions found in a printed book. When converting these images back into a printed bound book, the page sizes are standardized in ways that maintain the detail of the original. For large images, such as fold-out maps, the original page image is split into two or more pages.

Guidelines used to determine the split of oversize pages:

• Some images are split vertically; large images require vertical and horizontal splits.
• For horizontal splits, the content is split left to right.
• For vertical splits, the content is split from top to bottom.
• For both vertical and horizontal splits, the image is processed from top left to bottom right.

THE

HISTORY OF THE PARISH

OF

KINGTON ST. MICHAEL,

COUNTY OF WILTS.

BY THE

REV. J. E. JACKSON, M.A., F.S.A.,

Rector of Leigh Delamere, and Hon. Canon of Bristol.

DEVIZES:
PRINTED BY H. BULL, SAINT JOHN STREET.
M.DCCC.LVII.

THE

HISTORY OF THE PARISH

OF

KINGTON ST. MICHAEL,

COUNTY OF WILTS.

BY THE

REV. J. E. JACKSON, M.A., F.S.A.,

Rector of Leigh Delamere, and Hon. Canon of Bristol.

DEVIZES:

PRINTED BY H. BULL, SAINT JOHN STREET.

M.DCCC.LVII.

CONTENTS.

ILLUSTRATIONS.

Kington St. Michael.

By the Rev. J. E. JACKSON.

THE original name of this Parish was simply Kington. Upon its connection with Glastonbury Abbey it was called Kington Monachorum or Moyne: sometimes, from a Priory of Nuns settled here, Kington Monialium or Minchin Kington (Minchin being Saxon for Nun); and finally (about A.D. 1280) from the Saint to whom the Parish Church was then newly dedicated, Kington St. Michael.

Including the two large Tythings of Easton Piers and Kington Langley, the Parish contains 3950 acres, about 1300 inhabitants, and 220 houses. Easton Piers is in the Hundred of Malmsbury; the rest in that of North Damerham.

It lies about three miles north of Chippenham, the turnpike road to Malmsbury passing between the two villages of Kington St. Michael and Kington Langley, about three quarters of a mile from each. Eastward of this road the soil is chiefly Oxford clay: westward, cornbrash and Forest marble. The adjoining parishes are, on the north, Leigh Delamere and Stanton St. Quintin: on the west, Yatton Kaynell, and Allington (in Chippenham Parish); on the east, Draycote Cerne; and on the south, Chippenham and Langley Burrell. There is a small outlying portion of Kington called Peckingel on the bank of the Avon, between Langley Burrell and the Tithertons: and it has also three or four pieces of detached land between Allington and "The Long Stone," on the Marshfield Road.

As the name denotes, it was anciently crown property. In the year 934 King Athelstan bestowed a large portion of it upon Atheline one of his officers by a Deed,[1] in substance as follows:

---

[1] Printed in the New Monasticon, vol. i., Glastonbury: p. 59. Is the name of this Saxon officer to be recognized in that of the contiguous hamlet of Allington: scil. Atheline-town?

B

"I, ATHELSTAN, King of the Anglians, raised by the hand of the Almighty to the throne of all Britain, freely give to my faithful servant Atheline a certain portion of land, to wit, 15 cassates (*farms*) in a place called by the natives At Kingtone; to hold it with all rights, &c., thereto belonging, free from the irksome yoke of bondage, so long as he lives, to leave the same for ever at his death to any heir he pleases. If any one (which God forbid) swollen with insolence, shall dare to infringe or curtail in any matter great or small this my writ of gift, let him know that at the last day of Judgment when the Archangel's trumpet shall sound, he, together with the traitor Judas (called by the Sower's holy seed, the Son of perdition), and with all impious unbelievers who deny that on the altar of the Cross Christ took away the sins of the world, shall perish everlastingly in fiery torment.

This grant is made in the year of our Lord 934, at the town of Buckingham.

　　✝　ATHELSTAN, King, &c.
　　✝　CONSTANTINE, Viceroy, and many others."

A few years afterwards, Edmund the Elder, Athelstan's brother, by Deed dated at Chippenham A.D. 940, gave to his officer Wilfric 30 holdings *(mansiunculas)* at Langley: which is presumed to mean Kington Langley.[1]

MANOR UNDER GLASTONBURY ABBEY.

In the same reign (c. 941) the connexion of this manor with Glastonbury Abbey began by a donation of eight hides from the King, and of the 30 *mansiunculae* just mentioned, from Wilfric.[2]

In 987 the monks received a further and principal gift of 40 manses at Kington from Ethelred II., or the Unready, "to be by them held so long as the Catholic Faith should endure in England."

It was probably as a fee for this alienation and in order to secure the estate to the Church that a devout Lady, one Elswith wife of a nobleman called Elphean, paid to the crown 40 *mancuses*[3] of gold,

---

[1] The Deed, naming the boundaries, is in the New Monast. I. p. 60.
[2] New Mon. I. p. 4.
[3] From *manu-cusa*, coined with the hand.

For the same purpose she also purchased Merton in South Damerham.[1] King Ethelred's grant of Kington is witnessed by (the probable instigator to the gift) Dunstan Archbishop of Canterbury, afterwards Abbot of Glaston, and Oswald Archbishop of York. These donations were confirmed by the Popes, Lucius II. in 1144, and Alexander III. in 1168.[2]

From the Glastonbury charter and some other scources, a few notices of Kington have been gleaned, possibly interesting to local readers.

The only place under the name of Chintone in Wilts, mentioned in the Domesday survey, is an estate of no great extent then held by Ralph de Mortimer, a large owner in this neighbourhood. It had been held in the reign of the Confessor by one Alwin a Saxon, under the Church of Glastonbury. It is probable that the land alluded to was that afterwards given by the Mortimers to endow the Priory of Kington.[3] The principal estate of the Abbey of Glastonbury seems in the Domesday survey to be described under the name of Langleghe.[4]

The wood called Haywood, then much larger than it is now, belonged at this time partly to the Abbey, partly to one William of Haywood (now a farm house adjoining): and between these proprietors many disputes took place, according to documents which John Aubrey has copied.[5]

In other documents it is mentioned that the Abbot of Stanley had 40 acres at the western side of the Parish: and the Abbot of Malmsbury 21 acres, given to his house by William Wayte of Chippenham, and Edith his wife: doing service for the same to the Abbot of Glastonbury as Lord of the Fee.[6] Thomas Verdon was also a holder under the Church. The Prior and Convent of Monkton Farley (chief landowners in Allington) exchanged 22 acres near Fowleswyke Gate with the Abbot of Malmsbury.[7]

---

[1] New Mon. Glaston, No. C. and Sir R. C. Hoare's South Damerham, p. 3.
[2] Do. I. 37.   [3] Wyndham's Domesday, p. 389.
[4] Wyndham's Domesday, p. 109.   [5] Collect. for N. Wilts, I. 102.
[6] Malms. Chartulary, No. 218.
[7]   Do.   (Jones's) B. Mus. p. 110.

A.D. 1171. The Glastonbury estate here was let to farm at £8. From the small quantity of stock upon it, 24 oxen, 11 heifers, 26 pigs and 250 sheep, it is evident that very little of the parish was then enclosed.

About the year 1200 a violent commotion took place amongst the monks of Glastonbury, in consequence of an attempt on the part of the Crown to unite that Abbacy with the See of Wells. After a very long controversy, the matter was settled by the Pope's delegates, who decreed that though the two offices should remain distinct, a portion of the estates of the Abbey should be assigned to the Bishop of Wells. In this Kington was included. The controversy was revived on the succession of Bishop Jocelyn to the See of Wells, and was finally settled in 1218 by the restoration of Kington (with some others) to its former owners; but the Advowson was to remain with the Bishop.[1]

A.D. 1235-53. After the recovery of the Manor, Glastonbury Abbey being then under the government of one of its best Abbots, Michael of Ambresbury, Kington partook of the benefits of his administration. A fresh adjustment of Tithe, deranged during the late dispute, gave satisfaction to the inhabitants: a new grange was built, the Church restored, and Abbot Michael gave money to found an obit for himself and a charity to the poor. The charity and obit have of course long disappeared, but the village still unconsciously retains a reminiscence of this benefactor in the name which it bears: having selected from the calendar for its renovated Church one that should be also complimentary to the renovator.

The Historian of the Abbey, Adam of Domerham, says that about this time it was much in debt; an unfortunate predicament to which the improvements at Kington had perhaps contributed. For purpose of relief Abbot Robert of Pederton leased the Manor to one Robert Pentone for his life. The name of the lessee, when quickly pronounced, so nearly resembles that of the lessor as to make the transaction likely to have been a little family affair; for which, confirmation by the Pope was necessary, and was granted by Pope Alexander in 1258.

---

[1] New Monast. I. p. 5.

In 1266 the King granted to the Abbot and his successors in their Manor of Kington a Market every week on Tuesday, and a Fair there every year for three days, viz. :—on the eve, on the day, and on the morrow of St. Michael. Also Free Warren in all his demesne lands of the Manor of "Kington," so that no one should enter those lands to hunt therein, or to do ought which to the right of warren pertains, without the consent of the said Abbot or his successor, under a penalty of £10. Witnesses, William (Bitton) Bishop of Bath and Wells ; and others. The grant is dated at Kenilworth, 6 Nov. 51 H. III.[1]

In 1287 the Manor having again fallen into hand (probably by the expiration of Robert Pentone's term for life above mentioned), the Abbot and Convent applied to their own use the produce of their grange at Kington. Besides the sum of £160 a year allowed out of their general rental for the uses of the kitchen, the cook was to take 20s. a year out of the Manor of Kington, to be divided between himself and the "Pittancer." The total annual consumption of grain at the Abbey was 360 quarters of wheat, 338 of barley, and 920 of oats : of which quantity the bailiwick of Kington supplied during the six winter months 240 of wheat and barley and 50 of oats : during the summer 50 quarters of oats a week.

The Abbot of Glastonbury had certain jurisdiction and franchises throughout the scattered Hundred of which North Damerham forms a part. There was a chief Bailiff for the whole Hundred, to whom the Bailiff of North Damerham was responsible. These franchises were granted by charter of King Henry III.[2] : before which time the four parishes of Kington, Nettleton, Grittleton, and Christmalford (forming the principal part of North Damerham) seem to have been considered as in the Hundred of Chippenham. In 1321 Edmund Gascelyn, Lord of the Hundred of Chippenham formally by deed quitclaimed to the Abbot, all rights and profits of summons and distraint, &c., in these four parishes.

---

[1] Printed in New Monast. I. p. 45 : also Harl. Chart. 58. J. 22. Many of these notices of Kington are to be found in Bishop Tanner's Collection, Bodl. Lib. Oxford ; marked T.T. 342.
[2] Plac. de Q. W. p. 802.

The deed was dated Feb. 2, 14 Edw. II.[1] The Abbot's Hundred Court was held at Kington: and Aubrey has preserved a letter of apology for non-attendance, from one John of Artherne, (47 Hen. III.)[2]

1517-8. From a fine MS. volume in the British Museum (Harl. MS. No. 3961) containing a Terrar of the Glastonbury Estates in the time of Abbot Beere, 1517, the following extracts are taken, relating to their property at Kington. After special perambulation and measurement it was stated on the faithful report of Richard Snell the Præpositus or steward, John Tanner, Wm. Neck, John Kington, H. Gingell of Langley, and others, that

" Richard Snell the Lord's farmer held the Manor House *(curia dominicalis)* and about 320 acres; thereof 20 were in Peckingell mead, 20 in Moreshall, 30 in Ruydon *(Riding)*, paying to the Prioress of Kington as Rectress for certain feeding there 8s. 6d. per annum. Also 400 acres in Heywood. A common called Langley Heath, 310 acres, where the Lord and customary tenants intercommoned, with rights of common to Thomas Montague, John Gingell and their tenants in Langley.

" The Freeholders in Kington were John Saunders of Heywood, who held the land late Thos. Bolehide's *(now Bulidge)*, paying a couple of geese yearly of the value of 8d.; Thomas Tropenell, and the Prioress of Kington. The Abbot of Malmsbury also held as of this Manor a house in Malmsbury, late William Hall's.

" Amongst the customary Tenants were Isabel Russell, widow, for Syddelyate, La Nayshe, Culverwell; Wm. Neck of Langley, for James's Cross; Robert Colchester, for Stanton's Dene (the hollow between Swinley and Stanton Park); Thos. Stockman, for Peckinghull and some land lying beyond the Avon in Kayleway; John Bullock, for Peckinghull and Pennicroft, paying 12d. to the Lord and 6d. to the Prior of Bradenstock, and having a bed of hay allowed him; John Kington, for Ellenstubb near Easton lane end; Walter Amyatt, for Priday, Bydellwell and Vernalles cross; Robert Bell, for Hintelthorn, and many others.

" The Guardians of the Chapel of St. Peter at Langley held for 90 years half an acre of land round the said Chapel paying 2d. a year. The inhabitants of Kington had common in Heywood from 3 May to Feb. 2. The Lord's farmer to pay 3s. 6d. to the Vicar of the Parish Church, though the Abbot disputed the payment and considered that the Prioress was liable. It was particularly to be observed about the common called Langley Heath, that the farmer of the Lord of Langley Burrell and the Rector there claimed rights of common utterly unknown to the Abbot: also that the same Lord of Langley Burrell claimed xiid a year for a right of road from Pekinghull Mead to the Abbot's land in Kington,

---

[1] Printed in Aubrey's Coll. for N. W. I. 110.
[2] Coll. for N. Wilts, I. p. 106.

by what title was unknown. And the Prioress had the right of erecting gallows within that part of the Manor where her lands and those of the Abbot were intermingled."

AFTER THE DISSOLUTION.

In 1536 (27 Hen. VIII.) on the attainder of Abbot Whiting, an enquiry was made into the value of the Manor by Richard Pollard and Thomas Moyle :

" It was found to be worth in rents, free and customary, £23 17s. 3d. The Demesne farm £3 7s. 8d., besides 28s. for the Fee of Richard Snell, Bailiff there. Other casualties including 53s. 8d. for sale of wood, £5 0s. 1½d. Fines of land 20s. There was a wood of 300 acres (Haywood) chiefly of scrubbed and lopped oaks worth to be sold £142. The Timber of great oaks £20. 25 men in the Manor ready to serve the King, and two Bondmen both body and goods at the King's pleasure." *(Val. Eccl.)*

1540. (32 Hen. VIII.) Whilst the Manor was in the hands of the Crown the following return (in the Augmentation Office) was made of its profits and outgoings, by Richard Snell the Lord's Farmer and Bailiff.

" *Freeholders* paying quit rents, John Saunders, 8d. for the price of 2 geese for a tenement at Haywood, late Bolhides. Thomas Tropenell, for land late Baring's 5s. 9½d. The late Abbey of Malmsbury's land 10 pence.

" *Customary Tenants.* Richard Snell, 67s. 8d. for the Demesne Court, viz. : The Hall, Chamber, Kitchen, Grange, Barton, Dovecot, and Croft on the north side of the Court : besides having to repair all the houses in Kington, and to provide meet hay for the horses of the steward and their officers there, as well for the holding of the Courts as for the good governance of the Lordship. 10s. from the Toll of the Fairs there holden this year on the Feast of St. Michael. Total £23 6s. 3½d.

" *Lifeholders.* 16 pence for the rent of all shrouded oaks and other trees growing on the Lord's common called "Langley heath," and 10s. for the Agistment of the cattle of the Lord's Tenants in the wood called Heywood. Also for fees at the Courts, Heriots, and Strays. Total income £32 15s. 2d.

" The outgoings in wages to the steward and King's officers at the Courts of Kington, Grittleton, &c., as well as for the good governance of the Lordship, 53s. 2d. The Manor house and " Pounfold " were also repaired at the King's expense."

The Manor then became the property of the family who had been for some years its stewards, viz. :

SNELL OF KINGTON.

This name is an old Wiltshire word signifying "*sharp.*" "Roger commonly called Snell " of Allington, near Chippenham, occurs in

the list of the Vicars of Malmsbury, in 1312.[1]   By what peculiar
display of dexterity the Vicar of Malmsbury had earned the
cognomen, does not appear ; but, if Aubrey's tale be true, it was
one that fitted the Ex-bailiff of the Abbot's Manor of Kington
exceedingly well.   For he mentions a tradition as current at that
time in the village, that the Bailiff, foreseeing the Fall of the Abbeys,
and as a necessary consequence, the termination of his own services,
had followed the example of another unrighteous Steward on the
eve of dismissal, by providing for himself at his Master's expense.
He forgot (so the story went,) to settle with the Abbey for the latest
arrears of rent, and poor Abbot Whiting having something else
to think of than any balance there might be to his credit in his
Bailiff's books, Snell used that money in buying the estate.   The
purchase was made in 1543, for £803 17s. 2¼d.

By Letters Patent dated 22 April, 35 Hen. VIII. (1543), the
King granted to Nicholas Snell of Mychels Kyngton, gentleman,
all the Manor of Kyngton with all rights, together with Haywood
(220 acres), late part of the possessions of the Abbey of Glastonbury, to hold to him and his heirs for ever, paying yearly at
Michaelmas £3. 8s. 4¼d. to the Crown, and an annual fee of 16s. 8d.
to the Steward.[2]

The village would no doubt gladly cherish any malicious joke
against their new landlord ; first perhaps because he had been the
Steward and was now the Squire, but chiefly because, for his own
benefit, he deprived them of certain usages to which they had been
accustomed.   The Abbot's Park, or Demesne in hand, in which
was a large carp-pond, or rather several ponds in train, lay west of
the Church and Court-house, " extending round to the ditch in a
close called Ryding, north of the said house."   This seems to have
included the present Lodge farm, Haywood farm, and about 40

---

[1] Wilts Instit.

[2] See orig. grant, 35 Hen. VIII., Roll 121, part 3.   In the Chapter House
Fines, and in Harl. MS 760, p. 29, Sir Edward Darell is mentioned as having
died in 1549 seized of the Manor of Kington St. Michael, leaving William his
son and heir.   Possibly this may refer to some other part of the Parish.   The
Abbot's estate certainly belonged at that time to the Snells.

acres now Captain Clutterbuck's. The feeding was common to the Abbey tenants, and they also had certain parcels of land in the Westfield then unenclosed, between Kington and Draycote. The new owner wishing to enlarge his prospect and grounds shut them out of the Park and took away their Westfield allotments. "So," says Aubrey, "heretofore they had been able to keep a whole plough, but since, having only work enough for half a plough, they lived poorly and needily:" and probably wished the Abbot back again.

The first of this Kington family of Snell came from Biddestone, having married a Keynell, of an ancient house from which Yatton takes its name. After the step from Steward to Landlord, they were returned to Parliament, married well, and were Knighted. Nicholas the purchaser, was Sheriff of Wilts 1565: M.P. for Chippenham 1555, for the County 1557, and for Malmsbury 1570. He rebuilt the Court-house at Kington, which still remains, in a decayed condition, but presenting at the back (which was formerly the front) some architectural features not without elegance, in the Italian style then newly in fashion. Over the entrance on a stone shield is a cross flory, the arms of his family.[1] His grandson Sir Thomas Snell married a daughter of Sir Robert Long of Draycote. He was in the Navy, "a good astrologer," says Aubrey emphatically, "and a Captain in the Iceland voyage." He died 1612. His only son and successor Sir Charles Snell was one of the early associates of Sir Walter Raleigh : but on what sort of footing, and for what particular object, (not very creditable to so eminent a name,) we are informed by the same authority. "Sir Walter's companions in his youth were boisterous blades, but generally those

---

[1] The House is now the property of Mr. Coleman. The west front is surmounted by a very large carving in stone six foot high, representing birds eating out of a basket on a human head. Perhaps an allusion to the dream of Pharoah's butler, (Gen. xl. 17.) previous to his "head being lifted up from off him," and applicable here to the then recent and similar fate of Mr. Snell's predecessor and late master, Abbot Whiting. It was at this house Aubrey saw one of his wonders. "Having spoken of mists it brings to my recollection that in December, 1653. being at night in the Court of Sir Charles Snell's house at Kington St. Michael, there being a very thick mist, we saw our shadow on the fog, as on a wall, by the light of the lanterns, about 30 or 40 foot distance or more." *Nat. Hist. of Wilts, p.* 15.

that had wit, except otherwise upon designe to gett them engaged
for him : as for instance Sir Charles Snell of Kington St. Michael,
in North Wilts, my good neighbour, an honest young gentleman,
but kept a perpetual sott. Sir W. engaged him to build a ship (The
Angel Gabriel) for the designe for Guiana, w[h] cost him the
Manor of Yatton Keynell, the Farme at Easton Piers, Thornhill
and the Church Lease of Bps. Canning, w[h] ship upon Sir Walter's
attainder was forfeited."[1]   Sir Charles was further "famous for
having till the Civil Wars as good hounds for the hare as any were
in England for handsomeness and mouth (deep-mouthed) and
goodness, and suited one another admirably well."[2]   He was the
last male owner and died unmarried and intestate in 1651.   Upon
his death the Manor of Kington descended to his three sisters and
heirs-at-law, or their representatives.   A partition was made in
1656.   The three sisters were Mrs. Penelope Newman, Mrs. Barbara Stokes, and Mrs. N. Gastrell.

The eldest, Penelope, having died in her brother's lifetime, the
representatives claiming her third at the partition, were the families
of Sadler, Coleman, and Edward Stokes.   The Sadler's share, lying
at Allington and Peckingell, is now the property of their descendant
the Rev. Isaac Sadler Gale.   Mr. Walter Coleman of Langley, in-
herits his ancestor's portion.

The second sister Barbara, wife of Charles Stokes, also died in
her brother Sir Charles's lifetime.   In 1679 this undivided one third
was sold by her grandson John Stokes for £5500, to the Trustees
of the marriage of John Lawford, Esq., of Stapleton, Co. Glouc.,
and his wife Jane, daughter of Sir William Duckett.   In 1713 it
was again sold, to Mr. Ayliffe White, of a family fomerly of Langley
Burrell and Grittleton.   His grandson (of the same names,) dying
in 1826, his estate was purchased by Mr. R. H. Gaby, Mr. N.
Atherton, and Mr. W. Whitworth.   Mr. Atherton's house and
lands were again sold (1856) to Captain Hugh Clutterbuck, second
son of the late Thomas Clutterbuck of Hardenhuish, who now
resides at Kington.   The Lodge farm, late Mr. Whitworth's, has

---

[1] Lives of Eminent Men, II. 514.
[2] N. H. of Wilts, p. 60.

SNELL OF KINGTON ST. MICHAEL.

Arms, Quarterly gules and azure, over all a cross flory or.

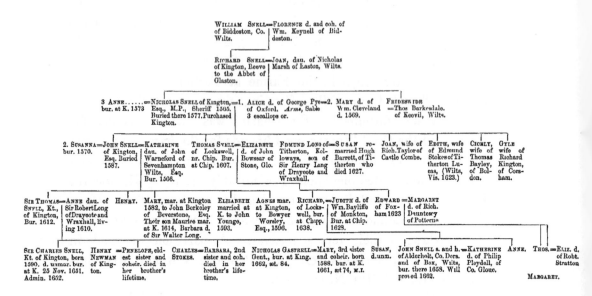

WILLIAM SNELL = FLORENCE d. and coh. of
of Biddeston, Co. | Wm. Keynell of Bid-
Wilts. | deston.

RICHARD SNELL = JOAN, dau. of Nicholas
of Kington, Reeve | Marsh of Easton, Wilts.
to the Abbot of |
Glaston. |

3 ANNE...... = NICHOLAS SNELL of Kington, = 1. ALICE d. of George Pye = 2. MARY d. of FRIDESWIDE
bur. at K. 1573 Esq., M.P., Sheriff 1565. of Oxford. *Arms*, Sable Wm. Cleveland = Thos Barkesdale.
  Buried there 1577. Purchased 3 scallops or. d. 1569. of Keevil, Wilts.
  Kington.

2. SUSANNA = JOHN SNELL = KATHARINE THOMAS SNELL = ELIZABETH EDMUND LONG of = SUSAN re- JOAN, wife of EDITH, wife CICELY, GYLE
bur. 1570. of Kington, dau. of John of Lockswell, d. of John Titherton, Kel- married Hugh Rich. Taylor of of Edmund wife of wife of
  Esq. Buried Warneford of nr. Chip. Bur. Bowssar of loways, son of Barrett, of Ti- Castle Combe. Stokes of Ti- Thomas Richard
  1587. Sevenhampton at Chip. 1607. Stone, Glo. Sir Henry Long therton who therton Lu- Bayley, Kington,
    Wilts., Esq.,   of Drayeote and died 1627.   cas, (Wilts, of Bol- of Cors-
    Bur. 1566.   Wraxhall.   Vis. 1623.) don. ham.

SIR THOMAS = ANNE dau. of HENRY. MARY, mar. at Kington ELIZABETH AGNES mar. RICHARD, = JUDITH d. of EDWARD = MARGARET
SNELL, Kt., Sir Robert Long 1582, to John Berkeley married at at Kington, of Locks- Wm. Bayliffe of Fox- d. of Rich.
of Kington, of Drayeote and of Beverstone, Esq. K. to John to Bowyer well, bur. of Monkton. ham 1623 Dauntesey
Bur. 1612. Wraxhall, liv- Their son Maurice mar. Younge, Worsley, at Chipp. Bur. at Chip.   of Potterne
  ing 1610. at K. 1614, Barbara d. 1593. Esq., 1596. 1638. 1628.
    of Sir Walter Long.

SIR CHARLES SNELL, HENRY = PENELOPE, eld- CHARLES = BARBARA, 2nd NICHOLAS GASTRELL = MARY, 3rd sister SUSAN, JOHN SNELL s. and h. = KATHERINE ANNE. THOS. = ELIZ. d.
Kt. of Kington, born NEWMAN est sister and STOKES. sister and coh. Gent., bur. at King. and coheir, born d.unm. of Alderholt, Co. Dors. d. of Philip   of Robt.
1590. d. unmar. bur. of King- coheir. died in   died in her 1662, æt. 84. 1588. bur. at K.   and of Box, Wilts. Pleydell, of   Stratton
at K. 25 Nov. 1651. ton. her brother's   brother's life-   1661, æt 74, M.I.   bur. there 1658. Will Co. Glouc.
Admin. 1652.   lifetime.   time.   proved 1662.

MARGARET.

descended (1857) to his son-in-law, William Peel, Esq., of Swindon Lodge, near Manchester.

The youngest of Sir Charles Snell's sisters, Mary the wife of Nicholas Gastrell, was living at the time of the partition in 1656. Her third share descended entire to her great grandson Jonathan Power, Esq., of Kington St. Michael, who died unmarried in 1748. Mr. Power's estate was apportioned under an Act of Parliament in 1783 amongst his four sisters. Haywood farm, the share of his eldest sister Margaret (wife of Wm. Clifford), is now the property of her descendants the Misses Mascall of Allington. The share of his second sister Elizabeth, Mrs. Gilpin, has since passed into various hands. The share of his third sister Rebecca wife of John Knott, was purchased by the late Joseph Neeld Esq., of Grittleton. And that of the fourth sister, Mrs. Sarah Coleman, including the old Grange or Manor House north of the Church, now forms a further part of the property of Mr. Walter Coleman of Kington Langley.

All the above were included in the estate formerly belonging to Glastonbury Abbey. The House in which Captain Clutterbuck lives is said by a doubtful tradition to have been a summer residence of the Abbot: and the hill near it, south of the Church, is still called "the Tor Hill," after the more celebrated one of that name at Glastonbury.

SWINLEY. (Swine-lea.)

Is a Farm on the N.E. side of the parish, divided from Stanton St. Quintin's by a grassy hollow called Stanton Dene, along which runs the boundary brook. It was held under Glastonbury by the Fitzurse family. A William Westbury, Hen. VI., had land here as also at a neighbouring farm called Whitman's (now Whitelands). Some Estcourts "of Swinley" were buried in Kington Church, 1706. The property was purchased by the late Mr. Neeld of Grittleton.

MORESHALL.

A smaller farm than the last, between Swinley and Leigh Dela-mere: probably takes its name from some ancient owner. An

Alice *More* was Prioress of Kington in 1431. Aubrey says it belonged to Kington Priory, but in the Schedule of the Estates of that House, only a field or two appear under this name. In 1700 it belonged to a Mr. Chapman; and in 1856 it was bought from the family of Burt by the late Mr. Neeld.

Langley, otherwise Kington Langley.

This hamlet is scattered over the high ground which forms the south east side of the Parish, and is traversed by 30 acres of common forming a pretty village green, skirted by farms, cottages, and gardens, and commanding an extensive view. The name of the Parish is prefixed to that of the hamlet, in order to distinguish it from Langley Burrell adjacent. Sometimes, for the same reason, it was called North Langley.

It has been already stated (p. 37,) that 30 households with their land were given here by the Anglo-Saxon King Edmund the Elder, to his officer Wilfric, about A.D. 940. The grant, which is a fair specimen of the style used in old monastic charters, (or at least in documents pretending to be such,) runs thus in translation :—

"✠ O Cross! that rulest over all Olympus, glorious foundation of the Throne of Christ our Lord, my Alpha and Omega, bless with thy mark the beginning, middle, and end of this writing. More brilliant than the stars and holier than all other gifts in the sight of Christ, thou hast endowed with largest privileges the Royal House of Edmund King of the Anglo-Saxons. This, Wilfric enriched by Sovereign bounty, is able to proclaim with truth, so that by the characters of this writing to all it may be made known :— viz., that the said King, under favour of God, in the nine hundred and fortieth year since the Virgin Mother presented her Divine progeny to the world waiting for the Holy Spirit, and in the second year of his reign, endows the said Wilfric with 30 tenements at Langley to himself and his heirs. . . . Let all therefore now ponder the wise saying of a Christian writer, 'Render O ye rich, unto Cæsar the things that are Cæsar's, and unto God the thing that are God's. Do works of piety and justice and you set an example to the Catholic

Church.' Confirmed by King Edmund to Archbishop Wulfhelm at the well known place called Chippenham."

By this favourite, on whom Grittleton and Nettleton were also bestowed, Langley was transferred to Glastonbury Abbey.

LANGLEY FITZURSE, OR FITZURSE FARM.

Under the Abbey a portion of Langley was held at the Conquest by Urso, founder of the Fitzurse family, who also held under the same Lords, Clapcote in Grittleton, and Swinley above mentioned, by service and payment of scutage. In 1221 his descendant Jordan Fitzurse, tired of paying scutage, and wishing to make his estate independent of the Monks, resisted their claim, but finally submitted. Some Deeds (copied by Aubrey) refer to transactions between this family and the Abbey, touching certain mills and ponds; and now and then a quarrel with the neighbouring lord of Langley Burrell about boundaries and rights of feeding.

From whatever other amiable qualities the Fitzurse family may have derived its name, a good affection towards Churchmen clearly was not one of them, if it is true, as always has been stated, that Reginald of that ilk was one of the assassins of Thomas á Becket.

Their principal tenement here is still recognized in the name of Fitzurse farm, now an ordinary house on the north side of the village green, but formerly one of greater pretension. In Aubrey's time it was an ancient building with a great hall; and a moat, of which there are some traces.

In Edward VI. it had passed into the hands of Thomas Montagu, one the Abbot's tenants; and from his representative William Montagu, Esq., it was bought about 1580 by Sir Owen Hopton, Kt., of a Suffolk family, Lieutenant of the Tower.[1] It came to Sir Ralph Hopton of Witham Friary, Co. Som., created, for his loyalty to Charles I., Baron Hopton of Stratton, Co. Cornwall.[2] He died

---

[1] Proceedings in Chancery, vol. II., p. 18. in a suit by Wm. Montagu against Sir Thomas Tasburgh and others, to discover deeds relating to this property, which had been settled (by Thomas Montagu) on him and his brothers.

[2] Sir Ralph was nearly blinded by an explosion of gunpowder at Marshfield after the battle of Lansdown; and was carried to Chippenham and thence to Devizes.

D

in 1652 leaving no children; and his uncle Sir Arthur Hopton, on whom the Barony was entailed, having predeceased him, his (Sir Arthur's) four sisters became his coheiresses,[1] from whom, or from whose representatives, it was bought in the middle of the 17th century by Mr. Bampfield Sydenham. From him it descended to the late Mr. Sydenham Bailey, to whose children it now belongs.

The greater part of the Glastonbury lands in Langley, now belong to Mr. Walter Coleman, whose ancestor obtained them by marriage with one of the representatives of one of the three sisters of Sir Charles Snell, the grantee at the Dissolution; as already mentioned.

In 1765 an estate in Langley belonging to Mrs. Maynard, who then resided at the old Manor House in Kington, was purchased from her Trustees, Charles Viscount Maynard, Dr. Thomas [Bishop of Winchester], and the Rev. Wm. Butler, by Sir James Long of Draycot. This is now the property of Viscount Wellesley.

A property of the Gingells, customary tenants under the Abbey in 1273, was sold in 1664 (being then worth £100 a year) to Samuel Martin.

At the Dissolution a large part of Langley, called "The Heath," was unenclosed. It is named in Abbot Beere's Terrier, as measuring 310 acres: and was common both to the Abbey tenants and the owner of Fitzurse Farm.

St. Peter's Chapel, Kington Langley.

This stood about the middle of the village, on the north side of the road: but had been converted into a dwelling before 1670. In Abbot Beere's Terrier (1517), it is stated that the wardens of St. Peter's Chapel at Langley, held of the Abbey for 90 years half an acre of ground, paying 2d. a year.

The village Revel used in old times to be kept on the Sunday following St. Peter's Day (29th June), and was, Aubrey says, "one of the eminentest Feasts in those parts. Old John Wastfield of Langley told him that he had been Peterman at St. Peter's Chapel in

---

[1] So the Peerage. But the Wilts Visitation, 1623, (see "Butler,") mentions Mary a daughter of Sir Arthur Hopton, and widow of — Gurney, of Co. Som., who married William Butler of Langley, son of Thomas Butler of Hanger, in Bremhill.

the beginning of Q. Elizabeth's reign." The "Peterman" seems to have been the person chosen by the parish at the festival of the Dedication of the Chapel, to collect money for charitable purposes. Such was the primitive custom at the yearly village feast, founded probably on a still more ancient precept: "Go your way, eat the fat, and drink the sweet, and send portions unto them for whom nothing is prepared." [Nehem. viii. 10.] These rural meetings, when dissociated from the religious character, lost one element of respectability; and a Wake or Revel (from the French *reveiller*, to waken), signifying originally a vigil, or night-fast, observed before the day of Dedication, is now obliged to be defined in our dictionaries, as a feast with loose and noisy jollity. Sometimes it leads to worse, and in the year 1822 Kington Langley Revel was the occasion of, what Aubrey might have called, one of the eminentest *riots* in those parts. Some offence having been given to the villagers at the feast by a party of young men from Chippenham, several meetings were afterwards held for the purpose of planning revenge, and it was ultimately resolved that a grand attempt should be made on the 7th of September. Accordingly in the course of that evening about 30 or 40 men assembled at Chippenham, and about half-past 10 o'clock commenced their outrage by appearing in the street armed with bludgeons, and attacking all who came in their way; Mr. Joseph Hall, a saddler, was so severely bruised as to expire within a few hours. Mr. Reynolds, a brazier, died shortly afterwards. Constables were knocked down and beaten, and in short not less than thirty-one men, women, and children were more or less wounded.

The hamlet contains a population of about 600 and is a mile and a half from the Parish Church. This distance from Clerical superintendence and the wholesome discipline of Church and School, having been found to produce the usual ill effect of ignorance and irreligion, testified by numerous and increasing cases brought before magistrates and boards of guardians, as well as by Sabbath breaking and irregularities of various kinds, the attention of the neighbourhood was called to the subject in the year 1853. By the exertions of some gentlemen, and especially Mr. E. L.

Clutterbuck of Hardenhuish, subscriptions were raised, and a new Church, bearing in recognition of the old Chapel the name of St. Peter, was built, and consecrated by the late Bishop of Gloucester and Bristol, on Thursday April 19th 1855. The site and £50 were given by Mr. Walter Coleman; £200 by the late Mr. Neeld of Grittleton; and the sums of £100 each by Mr. Clutterbuck, the late Rev. R. Ashe of Langley Burrell, Viscount Wellesley, and Mr. Sheppard. By further subscription a School has since been added, and a resident Curate is provided by the Vicar of Kington St. Michael's. Langley was sometimes called Langley Fearne (1513), or Langley Fernhill (1660).

St. Mary's Priory.

About three quarters of a mile north of Kington Church by the footpath leading to Leigh Delamere, in a pleasant open pasture-country, a very old farmhouse, with a heavily coped garden wall on on the eastern side, is the present representative of Priory St. Mary's. It was a House of Benedictines, for a Prioress, Sub-Prioress, and eight or nine Nuns, reduced to four at the Dissolution. Bishop Tanner quotes an authority to prove that it existed before A.D. 1155,[1] but neither the exact year of foundation, nor name of the Founder, have been positively ascertained. It was attributed in Aubrey's time to the Empress Matilda, mother of King Henry II., the founder of the neighbouring Abbey of Stanley near Chippenham. This may have been the case; but the charters of St. Mary's Priory, in which her name does not occur, seem to point out another person, one Robert of Bryntone, or as he is also called, "Robert, son of Wayfer of Brintone." Whether projected or not by some previous benefactor, he at least was the first to set the House up *(" locum constituit")*, by a gift of Tithes (in Dorset-shire) for maintenance: and the Nuns held the site by sufferance until it was formally assured to them by another of the family. Adam Wayfer of Brintone. The gift was confirmed by Sir Hugh de Mortimer, whose family, as already stated, held an estate in this

---

[1] " Pardon, monialibus de Chinton."—Rot. Pip. 2 Hen. II., *Wiltescire.*

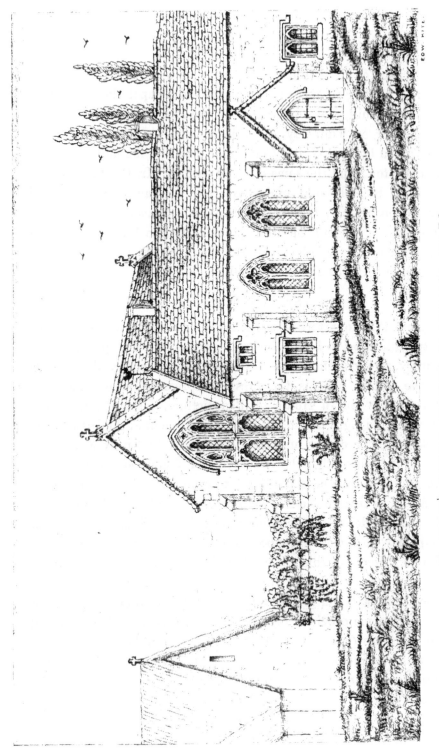

ST MARY'S PRIORY, KINGTON ST MICHAEL, WILTS.

[RESTORED FROM A SKETCH TAKEN BY JOHN AUBREY, ABOUT A.D. 1660.]

parish, of the Abbey of Glaston.[1]   In the Martyrology of the
Priory, a day was set apart for commemoration of " Adam de
Wayfer and the Mortimers, who gave us all our land in Kington."[2]

Besides the land, they had also the Rectorial Tithe, and presented to the Vicarage.   The Rectory originally belonged to
Glastonbury Abbey, but under the arrangement before alluded to
(p. 39,) it was transferred to the See of Bath and Wells, and then
given to the Nuns by Robert Burnell, Bishop.

Their estate lay chiefly about the House ; including more than
now forms the Priory Farm. Amongst their outlying property were
the granges of Studley near Calne, and Cadenham, with Tithes
there and at Redmore, given by Alexander of Studley ; the Rectory of Twerton, near Bath, by Wm. Malreward ; a Manor at
Great Somerford, (held by a chief rent under the Earl of Arundell,
at the Dissolution,) given by Richard de Heriet ;[3] land at Bradley,
near Alton, Hants, by Petronilla Bluet ; Tithes at Stures and
Sanford, Lazarton and Stapleton, near Stourpayne, Dorset, by Wm.
of Harptree and Roger Villiers ; besides certain tenements at
Malmsbury, Sherston Parva, Uffcot, Leigh Delamere, (where a
small field adjoining the Rectory garden still bears the name of
" The Minchery,") Calne,[4] and Boyton, Co. Wilts ; Cam and Dod-
dington, Co. Gloucester.   To stock their home farm, Wm. de
Longespee, Earl of Sarum, gave them by will in 1225, 100 ewes
and 6 cows.   The coppice between the Nunnery and Easton Piers

---

[1] The Priory continued to pay a chief Rent to Glastonbury till the Dissolution.
(*Val. Ecc.*)

[2] The Brimpton alluded to is in Berkshire, a few miles south of Reading. In
one of the Priory Charters (No. 7), several places in that neighbourhood are
named as of the estate of Mortimer, and at Brimpton itself the fourth part of a
Fee held under Edmund de Mortimer belonged to these very Nuns, (I. p. M.
IV. 87.) Though little is known of this family of Wayfer, still as they assumed
the name of " Brintone" from their residence, it is clear that they were terri-
torial clients there as here, of the great House of Mortimer.   Their name is also
met with in that capacity, in Salop.   In later times a Roger Mortimer, who
died 1336, married a daughter of Sir Robert de Wafre ; and in A.D. 1349, a
Richard Wayfer was Rector of Luckington, about six miles from Kington.

[3] The Nuns had also some Tithe in Little Somerford.

[4] For their land and Tithe there, they paid an acknowledgement of two
pounds of wax per annum to the Churchwardens of Calne.

was given by the owner of that Manor, Sir John of Easton, to pray for the souls of himself and family.

Below this coppice, and beyond a rivulet south of the Priory, in a field called the Minchin meadow were their fishponds. And on the east side of the House was a large ground called the Nymph Hay,[1] where the Sisters with their young scholars used to take exercise. In his remarks upon Nunneries as places of education, Aubrey thus describes their appearance :—

" The young maids were brought up, (not at Hackney, Sarum Schools, &c., to learn pride and wantonness,) but at the Nunneries, where they had examples of piety and humility, modesty and obedience, to imitate and practice. Here they learned needlework, the art of confectionary, surgery, [anciently no apothecaries or surgeons : the gentlewomen did cure their poor neighbours : their hands are now too fine]; physic, writing, drawing, &c.   Old Jacques, who lived where Charles Hadnam did, could see from his house the Nuns of the Priory of St. Mary's, Kington, come forth into the Nymph-Hay with their rocks and wheels to spin, and with their sewing work.   He would say that he hath told threescore and ten, but of Nuns there were not so many, but in all, with Lay-Sisters, as widows, old maids, and young girls, there might be such a number. This was a fine way of breeding up young women, who are led more by example than precept : and a good retirement for widows and grave single-women to a civil, virtuous, and holy life.   In the old hedges belonging to the Priory were " (and still are) " a good number of Barberry trees, which t'is likely the Nuns used for confections.   Their last priest[2] was Parson Whaddon,

---

[1] Now corrupted into " Empty."   Names, like the coin of the realm, suffer by currency ; and every parish map is rich in riddles which it is by no means easy to solve.   Such as " Izell's " from *East-hills*, " Vanity-field " from *Wal-nut-tree-field*, " Marriage Park " (near Malmsbury,) from *Mauduit's Park*, " Crawlboy's wood " from an old Norman name *Croile-bois*.   A copse on Bedwyn common planted whilst Lord Ailesbury was travelling in Sicily, and called, in order to mark its age, the " *Sicilian* " plantation, is now " Thistle-hand."

[2] The Priory had a Priest to perform Divine Service from the time of its foundation, with a stipend of £5 6s. 8d., nearly equal to the whole Tithes of the Rectory £6 13s. 4d. (*see Val. Eccl.*)

whose chamber is that on the right hand of the Porch with the old fashioned chimney."

There is an engraving of the remains of the Nunnery in the Gent. Mag. 1803, p. 717. On the eastern side of it was a square Court, the north wing of which was a Chapel. This had a Norman doorway, but transomed windows.[1] It fell to decay soon after the Dissolution, but a few arches were standing in 1800. In the terraced garden freestone coffins have been occasionally found; and in one grave which, by the chalice discovered in it, had been that of a priest, a stone of the thickness of a grinding stone having in the centre a heart held between two hands.

The Editors of the New Monasticon had never met with any impression of the Seal of this Priory.

NAMES OF PRIORESSES OF ST. MARY'S, KINGTON,

Collected from Deeds, Registers, and the Book of Obits kept in the Nunnery.

A.D.

	ELEANOR	Mentioned in Aubrey's MSS.
c. 1280.	CLARICIA	Priory Charter, No. xi. *(see infra.)*
. . .	EDITH OF BRISTOW . .	Book of Obits, 26 Dec.
. . .	AMICE	Do. do. Nov. 10.
. . .	CHRISTINA CHARLTON .	Do. do. January 4.
. . .	CECILIA	Lambeth Reg. Reynolds.
1319.	JOAN DUREDENT . .	Resigned 8 March, 1325. Obit kept 21 Mar. [Lamb. Reg. Reynolds.]
1326.	DIONYSIA "of Horsehill under Chobham, in Surrey."	A Nun of Bromhale, near Windsor; made Prioress by the Archbishop of Canterbury. Lamb. Reg. Reynolds.
. . .	ISABEL HUSEE . . .	Obit kept 27 March.
1349.	LUCIA PAAS	
1431.	ALICE MORE	Late Sub-Prioress, Obit kept 2 Ap.
1434.	JOAN DONYTON or DYNGTON.	Obit 21 March.

---

[1] Aubrey has preserved the pattern of this window in his unpublished MS. called "Chronologica Architectonica."

. . . SUSANNA	Obit 23 May.	
. . . ALICE HANKERTON . .	Do. 11 June.	
. . . CHRISTINA NYE . .	Died 1454. Obit kept 2 Dec.	
1454. ALICE LAWRENCE . .	Resigned 1492. Sarum Register.	
1492. KATHARINE MOLEYNS .	A Professed Nun of Shaftesbury, elected 2 April. Sar. Reg.	

The Names of the Nuns at Kington in the time of Katharine Moleyns, Prioress, were

Joan Bristow.	Joan Hodges.	Agnes Burnell.
Alice Mershefeld.	Christina Westbourne.	Mulier Chynne.
Alice Lawrence.	Christina Woodland.	Alice Hawkins.

1506. ALICE STAUNTON . .	A Nun of this house: appointed Prioress by the Bishop, by lapse. Audley Reg. Sarum.
1511. CICELY BODENHAM . .	Afterwards Abbess of Wilton.

About this time happened the abduction of a Prioress by a very troublesome clerk at Castle Combe, as related in Mr. Poulett Scrope's History of that parish, p. 297. Sir John Scrope (who died 1517) in a supplication to the Archbishop of Canterbury, sets forth at great length sundry grievances endured by him at the hands of *Sir* Thomas Kelly, curate under *Sir* Ingeram Bedyl, the Rector: amongst which "he prayeth to be recompensed for his wrongful trouble and vexation that he hath had by the menes of the said Thomas Kelley, that *robbed the poor Monastry of Kyngton,* and *carryed away the Prioress* of the same." Cicely Bodenham was of a family settled at Bodenham in the Hundred of Downton. In the stained Chancel window, given by herself to Kington Church, Aubrey says there was remaining in his time, the greater part of her Picture in her cope and robes.

1534. ELIZABETH PEDE . .	Val. Eccl.
. . . MARY DENNIS . . .	

Of an old family at Pucklechurch. She was the last Prioress, and was pensioned with £5 a year. Aubrey's statement that "she died in Somerset within the memory of man," is corroborated by a note written on the fly-leaf of a Manuscript in Corpus Christi Coll. Oxford, [No. ccxx. fol. 3. b.] "This boke was appertaining to

Marye Dennis sometyme Ladie Abbesse of a certain Nunnery in Glostershyre [*read, Wiltshire*]: She dyed in Bristowe 1593, a good olde maide, verie vertuose and godlye: and is buried in the church of the Gauntes on the Grene."

The Convent was subject to the authority of the Bishop of Sarum both as Diocesan and Visitor. Under his license they elected their own Prioress, and presented her to the Bishop. If any thing in the election was found to have been uncanonical, it was annulled, and the Bishop then nominated. If properly conducted, it was confirmed, a mandate was issued to the Archdeacon to install the new Prioress, and a formal declaration of submission by her and the Convent was duly made, signed, and sealed with the mark of the cross.[1] The Nuns did not like the visitation of the Bishop and his Officers; and were desirous of having for their Patron the Abbot of Glastonbury: he being the Head of the First House of *Regulars*, of the same Religious Order as themselves (Benedictine), and moreover their own Landlord in chief. A curious story is told in some Deeds in the Registry at Sarum,[2] of a bold attempt to dispense with the Bishop's right of superintendance, made by one of these Ladies, Dame Alice Lawrence, Prioress in 1454. She permitted a certain Irish Franciscan friar, whose name is lost, to forge a Latin document purporting to come from Rome, by which the Priory was released from the inspection of the Diocesan, and transferred to the care of the Abbot. Of course as soon as the Bishop's right was denied, he applied to Rome, and the fraud was discovered. Dame Alice was quietly admonished to send in her resignation: but as she was considered to have been the dupe of the Franciscan friar, her sentence was lenient, and she was allowed to continue in the House in the rank of a Nun.

The following is the substance of the Latin Deeds that relate to this transaction :—

1. THE FORGED DOCUMENT : *purporting to be a Rescript from Pope Innocent VIII., A.D. 1490, addressed to the Abbot of Glastonbury,*

---

[1] See "Audley" and "Mortivale" Registers.
[2] "Langton" Register.

E

transferring to him from the Bishop of Sarum, the rights of Visitor over Kington Nunnery.

" Innocent, &c., to our beloved son, the Abbot´of St. Mary of Glastonbury of the Order of St. Benedict, in the Diocese of Wells, greeting:

" The circumspect anxiety of the Holy See is cheerfully directed to such measures as may usefully administer to the wants of Religious Persons. And to such as are most eminent for virtue and merit, it more particularly extends the favour of its protection.

" On behalf of our beloved Daughter Alice Lawrence, the Prioress, and of the Convent of St. Mary of Kington, of the Order of St. Benedict, in the Diocese of Sarum, a Petition lately sent to us sets forth, that, whereas it hath been the ancient custom for the Bishop of Sarum to visit that Monastery for the purpose of reforming manners and correcting vices ; his suite of horsemen and attendants upon those occasions is so great, that the means of the Monastery are unable to bear the expense thereby occasioned. That this hath happened, not once only, or in the regular course of the Visitation of the Diocese, but as often as he likes. That the Cells and other private apartments, appropriated to prayer and the use of the Nuns, are required for the accommodation of a number of secular attendants : and that the Bishop at pleasure supplies the Monastery with a chaplain of his own nomination, whensoever and whomsoever he may chuse.

" And whereas it has been further represented unto us, that, if the Convent is withdrawn from the visiting jurisdiction of the Bishop, and is placed under that of a Prelate Regular for the correction of faults and instruction in morals, the Prioress and Convent will be able to serve God more securely and quietly, and the frequent offences that arise out of its subjection to secular persons will in future be avoided :

" We therefore, desiring to entertain this application favourably, and exonerating the said Alice from all penalties, &c., &c., do hereby order, that you (the Abbot) summon the Parishioners of Kington and all others whom it may concern, and inquire diligently into the truth hereof. And if these allegations are founded on truth, that you forbid, by our authority, all opposition on the part of the said Parishioners: and that you collate and assign unto the said Alice the Priory whereunto belongeth cure of Souls, the annual value whereof doth not exceed, as she declareth, 36 marks sterling: and that you do induct her into corporal possession thereof, and when inducted, protect her, in all her rights until her death.

"No previous grant or privileges to the contrary withstanding, whether made to the Priory, or the Bishop and Chapter of Sarum: as to election, &c., &c.

"And that the said scandals, occasioned by the superintendence of secular officers, may for the future be put an end to, we decree that the Convent be exempt from all Episcopal Jurisdiction whatsoever, and be forthwith subject to your's.

"Likewise, we empower you once every three years, or more frequently, if desirable, to visit the said Monastery for the correction of morals; reforming whatever may seem to you to require reformation. And if our Reverend Brother the Bishop of Sarum shall again interfere with the same, let him know that he will incur the wrath of the Almighty, and of the Apostles Peter and Paul.

"Given at Rome 28th June, A.D. 1490, and the 6th of our Pontificate."

The Bishop of Salisbury having apprized the Court of Rome of the Forgery, received the following instructions:—

2. *The Pope to the Bishop of Salisbury.*

"To our venerable Brother greeting. Whereas we have lately received a copy of certain Letters purporting to have been issued by us at the instance of Alice Lawrence, Prioress of Kyngton, and have carefully inspected the same: which Letters it is your desire should be recalled and pronounced to be, as they most palpably are, surreptitious: whereof a copy is now enclosed to you with these presents:

"We, being anxious to investigate the matter thoroughly as we are bound to do, bid you endeavour by every means to obtain possession of the original Letters themselves and send them to us, and also ascertain by whom the despatching of them was contrived, with such other information as you can procure. Also that you compel any person detaining them, or otherwise offering impediment, to give them up and bear testimony to the Truth, under pain of Ecclesiastical censure. For which purpose, if need be, you will call in the aid of the Secular power.

"Given at St. Peter's, Rome, under the Séal of the Fisherman, 27 July, 1491."

3. *The Answer of Thomas Langton, Bishop of Salisbury, to the Pope.*

"Most Holy Father: After our humblest commendation and devout kisses of your Holiness's blessed feet; I received your Letter enclosing the copy of the document purporting, &c., and conveying your Holiness's orders. Whereupon I so proceeded against the Prioress and other suspected parties, as to obtain possession of the original document, which I herewith send to your Holiness. The name of the person who hath contrived this matter I have not been able to discover; excepting that he is said to be a certain Irish Friar, of the Order of St. Francis. But if I shall be able to discover where he is, whether in England or in Ireland, I promise my best exertions to arrest and detain him until I shall receive your Holiness's further instructions. Our Lord whose Vicegerent upon earth you are, have your Holiness in his blessed keeping.

"Given at London, 10 Novemb., 1491, by your most devoted Son, Thomas Langton, Bp. of Sarum."

4. *Alice Lawrence, the Prioress, being compelled to resign, the Bishop of Sarum appoints a new Prioress.*

"Thomas, by Divine permission, Bp. of Sarum, to our beloved Daughter the Lady Katharine Moleyns, Nun of the Monastery of Shaftesbury of the Order of St. Benedict, greeting. Whereas the Priory of Kington is vacant by the free resignation of Alice Lawrence; and the Sub-prioress and Convent have voluntarily solicited me, and conveyed to me as the Ordinary and Diocesan all their power in nomination of a successor; we, therefore, having heard of you a good report, &c., do elect you Prioress thereof, and by these presents depute to you in the Lord, the care and administration of all goods spiritual and temporal: reserving the rights and dignity of us and our Cathedral Church. In witness whereof we have affixed our Seal, at our Manor of Remmesbury, 9 April, 1492."

Then follow two other Mandates, one to the Archdeacon of Wilts for installing the New Prioress; and the other to the Sub-prioress and Convent, to receive and obey her.

Liber Obitualis.
The Book or Kalendar of Obits of Kington St. Mary's Priory.

Being a Register of Founders, Brethren,[1] Sisters, and others, Benefactors, whose names were appointed to be mentioned in the Prayers of the Convent upon the Days of their respective Deaths. Drawn out anew by KATHARINE MOLEYNS, Prioress there: in Lent 1493. (9 Hen. VII.)

(To the Obituary are prefixed copies of the following Formularies.)

I. "The ORDER to resseyve Brothers and Sisters and the suffrages of the Religious there.

II. "The ORDER to resseyve a Minchin there."

(The above are too long for insertion. The next is translated from the Latin.)

III. "Commendations to prayer in the Conventual Chapter for Benefactors living or dead."

"For the Living."

"I commend to you, amongst the living, the Chief Pontiff . . . . and all the Cardinals, the Archbishop of Canterbury, the Bp. of Sarum our Ordinary, the Bishop of Winton, the Abbot of Glaston, the Abbess of Shaftesbury, and all our Convent: specially them that labour and serve in our Church. Likewise the well being of all who give a helping hand to our Lord. Likewise" [A. B., the particular person whose Obit was kept].

---

1 The Chaplain was the only "Brother" resident in the House: but it was the custom to pay to influential friends, lay as well as clerical, the compliment of making them Honorary Brethren: or, as the phrase ran, "admitting them into the Fraternity of the Convent." See in the Book of Obits, under January 12.

2 From the Manuscripts of John Moore, Bishop of Ely, purchased at his decease by King George I., presented by him to the University of Cambridge, and now in the Public Library there. A list of ancient and forgotten names is not perhaps in itself of much importance; but as a sample of a class of Monastical Records not often met with, a "Book of Obits" may not be wholly void of interest.

"For the Dead."

"I commend to you, amongst the deceased, the souls of the Bishops of Sarum: of Reginald, late Bishop of Bath," (Fitz Jocelyn, 1191.) "of Savaric," (1205.) "late Bishop of Bath and Glastonbury, of Robert Burnell, late Bp. of Bath" (1292.) "of Adam son of Waifer of Kyngton, of Roger and Sir Hugh Mortimer: likewise the souls of all whose goods have been bestowed to the benefit of our House, and whose names are contained in the following Kalendar: likewise the souls of all the faithful deceased."

The Kalendar of Obits.

January.

iv. For the soule of Christine Charleton, late Prioress of Kyngton.

vii. For the soules of Adam sonne of Waifere of Kynton,[1] Roger Mortymer, and Sir Hugh Mortymer, that gave us all our lands in Kyngton.

viii. For the soules of the Bps. of Saulesbury, our special Benefactors and Ordinaries.

ix. — of Reynold Bp. of Bathe,[2] that gave us our Parsonage of Twyverton: and for the soules of Savary late Bp. of Bathe and Glaston: and of Jocelyn late Bp. of Bathe, that confirmed to us, by their writing, the same.

x. — of Robt. Burnell late Bp. of Bath, that gave us an Acre of lande in Kyngton and the Parsonage there.

xii. — of John Buttelar of Badmintone magna,[3] who was admitted into the Fraternity of this house.

xiii. — of Maud Osprynge.

xv. — of Maister Wm. Barker, late Parson of Sherston.

xvii. — of William of Salford and of Edith his wife, and of John Clayfield.

xxi. — of Mary, late Lady of Eston.[4]

xxii. — of Geffrey of Bathe.

xxvi. — of William of Abyngdon.

---

[1] The Founder of Kington Priory.

[2] Reginald Fitz Jocelyn, d. 1191. But in the Priory charter No. viii. Wm. Malreward is named as the donor of Twerton.

[3] The Butlers were anciently owners of Badminton.

[4] Easton Piers, contiguous to the Priory Estate.

FEBRUARY.

    v. — of Wm. Rowdon.[1]

    vii. — of Sir John Delamere, Kt.[2] and Johan his wyfe.

    xii. — of Elys of Milborne.

    xvi. — of Clemence Husee, Minchin of Kyngton.

    xviii. — of Sare of Sellye.

    xix. — of Hawyse of Lobenam.

    xx. — of Rafe Blewet.

    xxiv. — of Wm. Eston.

xxviii. — Joan Durdeyne, Mynchyn of Kyngton.

MARCH.

    i. For the Soules of Harry Hardynge.

    vii. — John, late Abbot of Malmsbury. — of Harry, late Monke of Bath. — of Agnes, Sub-prioress of Kynton.

    xii. — of Agnes Wellyshote : Mary Willys. — Agnes Wyngton, Minchen here.

    xiv. — of John Persay. — John Bradeley.

    xv. Memorandum : That the Altar in the Church of Kyngton was dedicated in honour of the Holy Mother of our Saviour, by Ralph [*meaning probably Robert*] Bp. of Sarum, on 15th March, A.D. 1435.

xviii. For the Soul of Maister Rych of Abingdon. — and of Walter Herrys.

    xix. — Julian Byshop.

    xxi. — Joan Dyngton, late Prioress here.

    xxiii. — Mawde Nethelton. — Isabel Warrener.

    xxiv. — Peter de Eston. — Robert and Geffrey.

    xxv. — Sir John Mortimer, and Harry. John Baker[3] of

---

[1] Probably Rowdon in Chippenham Parish.

[2] Of Leigh Delamere : living about A.D. 1290. He witnesses the Priory charter, No. xi.

[3] In the Obituary at the foot of the page of "March," are the following entries : " In the days of Dam Kateryne Moleyns Prioress here, John Baker gave to this House at Minchyn Kyngton,

    A Bone of St. Cristopher closed in cloth of gold, a noble Relyke.

    Thys boke, for to be their Mortiloge.

    A Boke of Seynts Lyves yn Englishe.

    A Spruse Table and a Cubbord that be in their parlor.

Briggewater, and Joan his wife were admitted Brother and Sister of this house on Lady Day, A.D. 1498. (*see below, Jun.* 27.)

xxvii. — Isabell Husye, late Prioress of Kyngtone. — Rafe Melkesham.

xxviii. — Julyan Hayes: Symon of Overton: Thomas Mounte, Chanon of Wells.

xxxi. — Henry Grafton.

APRIL.

   i. For the Soules of Johan Ingram.

   ii. — Alice More prioress of Kington: William Bradley and Margaret Montforde.

   v. — William Beames.

  vii. — Johan Malesyn.

   x. — Johan Berleye: Agnes Browne.

  xi. — Johan, Prioress of Kington, — of Sybil Dyxton: of Herry Beauforde (The Cardinal and Bp. of Wynchester) who died A.D. 1448.

  xii. — John Rose, and Agnes his wife.

 xiii. — Thomas Whittokesmede; of Roger Beverley, and Alice his Wyfe.

  xx. — Jordan of Holdesweyl. — Thomas Bek.

 xxiv. — Thomas Devant.

 xxvi. — Charile of Bytton: of Vincent Farthyn.

MAY.

   i. For the Soules of Maude Culham.

   ii. — Cristyne Cogan.

  iv. — Henry of Harnhull.

The mendyng and renewyng of an old Mas Boke of theirs.

A Fetherbed, a bolster, a Pylow, and 2 fair Coverlettes: The half of the money that was paid for the Ymage of Seynt Savyor stonding upon the Auter for their quire. And for the Ymages of St. Mighel and St. Kateryne in St. James's Chapell. Also the Aulter Cloth of the Salutacyon of oure Lady, being in St. James's Chapell: and 3 yards of Canvass annexed thereto to lye upon the Auter. A Tester and a Seller (*i e, a celler or canopy, ciel de lit*) that hangeth over my Lady's Bed. A Grail. A fair Matyns Boke, with Dirige and many good Prayers. A dozen of round pewter dishes with heires." (*ears?*)

vii. — Dame Johan of Eston : Alianore Baverton.

viii. — John Thornebyry.

ix. — Alexander Stodeley.[1]

x. — Sir Robert Huys.

xi. — Geffrey Scott and Isabell his wife.

xiii. — Walter Frary (or Tracy).

xiv. — John Bradeley.

xxiii. — Susanne, Prioress of Kington. — Raynold Jacob.

xxvii. — Agnes Walyngford.

xxviii. — Moryce, Monk of Farlye.

JUNE.

vii. For the Soules of Richard Comene.

xi. — Thomas Knapp and Avyce his wyfe. Also of Dame Alice Hankerton, Prioress of Kington.

xiii. — Adam Milton.

xvii. — Philippe of Sutton.

xx. — Rafe of Eston.

xxi. — John Milton and Alianor Barle.

xxiv. — Dame Cristina Westbourne.

xxvi. — Gilbert Derby.

xxvii. — of Richard Elys Baker,[2] Joan his wife, Thomas Baker, and Johan his wyfe : John Baker, and Joan, Margaret and Joan, his wyves. John Vicary, and Agnes his wyfe. Richard Clopton, and Alice his wyfe. Maister Will. Baker, late Parson of Petworth in Sussex.

xxix. — of John Zenar (?)

JULY.

i. For the Souls of Alyce Original ;[3] and Johan Grafton.

vii. — John le bon.

viii. — Margery Combe. — Adam Wellishot.

xiii. — Robert Helys.

---

[1] The Donor of Tithes, &c., at Studley, Cadenham, &c., see Charter x.

[2] An instance very rare at so early a period, of *two* Christian names.

[3] So spelled in the MS. copy from which this is taken, in the writing of Mr. James Gilpin, Recorder of Oxford, and a native of Kington. The real name was perhaps Elias Orescueil, a benefactor. See Charter xiii.

F

xvii. — Hawys of Abyngdon.

xix. — Nicholas Dyraunt ?

xx. — Thomas Martyn.

xxiii. — Robert Russell and Margaret his wyf.

xxvii. — John Byret ?

AUGUST.

    i. For the Soules of Martyn Wynterburne, Symon Fraun ceys, and John Hawyse.

viii. — Walter Boldry and Joan his wyfe.

  x. — Walter Charleton.

 xi. — John of Laverton.

xii. — Agnes Milton.

xiii. — Isabell Fryng, Robert Streffe and Alyce his wyfe, Mr. Wm. Streffe, Chanon of Sarum; of Crystine Joan, and Joan.

 xv. — Robert Turle; John Horton.

xviii. — Wm. Apilforde and Sara his wyfe.

xxij. — Gaffrey de Boys.

xxiv. — Johan late wyfe of John Baker.

xxvi. — Margaret Vyse : and Thomas her husband.

xxxi. — John Heyway and Isabell his wyfe.

SEPTEMBER.

    i. For the Soules of Joan Overton.

  ii. — Jordan le Warre : Mr. Robt. Bluntesdon.

 iii. — Mary Excester: Wm. Evesham: and Cristine his wyfe.

vii. — Richard Hawkesbury, Monk of Malmesbury: Johan late wyfe of Richard Elys Baker.

 xi. — Walter Jewne.

xiv. — William of Sutton.

xvii. — Maute of Abyndon. — Johan Nele.

xviii. — Sir Richard Awringe.

xxi. — Roger Helys. — and Katerine Wilkyns,

xxii. — Ide Cosyn.

xxiii. — Roger Stodeley. — Alexander Welyngton.

xxvii. — Wm. Wykam, late Bp. of Winchester.

xxviii. — Rosa Hylle, and John ———.

xxix. — Isabell of Westrop. — John Coldam.

xxx. — Katerine Hundredere ?

OCTOBER.

ii. For the Soules of Hely of Stodeley and Thos. Malemeys.

vi. — Richard Spenser.

vii. — Hugh Rementon.

xi. — John of Welitton.

xiv. — Sir Water Clopton, Kt.

xvi. — Nicholas Samborne, — and Nicholas his Son.

xviii. — Richard Tomelyne, Vicar of Kyngtone.

xxiii. — Margaret Selyman : — Katerine Swindon.

xxviii. — Elys of Calne.

xxix. — Maude Rementon.

NOVEMBER.

i. For the Soules of Gilbert Overton.

ii. — Margaret Baker: John Welliscote, — Gilbert Berewyke.

iii. — Alice Boydon.

vii. — Richard Inveyne (?)

viii. — Alice Turneys, — Johan, wyfe of Thos. Martyn.

x. — Amice Prioress of Kington, — Sir Hugh Mortymer. — Dunage Sottacre. — of Perys. — of Haveryng. — of Johan Martet.

xi. — Lady Joan Bristow.

xiii. — Geffrey Abbot of Glaston : (Fromont died 1322.)

xiv. — Luce, Byshop of ———.

xix. — Joan, wyfe of Thos. Baker of Lamport. — Sir Rob. Charleton Kt.

xxi. — John Scutte.

xxiv. — Edward of Pury. — Elene atte Pury.

xxvi. — John Bradeley. — Roger Stodeley.

xxviii. — Agnes Comerweyle.

DECEMBER.

i. For the Soules of Thos. Tanner.

iii. — Isabel Burley.

v. — Kateryne, wyfe of Nicholas Fortresbury.

vi. — Edmund Husce.

vii. — Thos. Wyleshete. — Joan Wynterburn. — Cristine Nr~ Prioress of Kington, who died A.D. 1454.

viii. — John Kynsman, Husbonman, — and Lady Alice Hare.

xi. — John Hance.

xii. — Gyles Bp. of Sarum, (G. de Bridport, consecrated at Canterbury 1256, died 1262.)

xiv. — Ely, late wyfe of Alexander Stodeley.

xvi. — William, Vicar of Kington. — Dame Alice Hardyng, Mynchyn of Lacock.

xviii. — Mr. Robert Gray.

xix. — Alice Mann.

xx. — Sir William of Lomene.

xxi. — Margaret Burley.

xxii. — John Adeneyte.

xxiij. — Agnes Delamere.

xxiv. — Sir — Turketill : Edith, a Mynchyn here.

xxvi. — Edythe of Bristow (Prioress).

xxx. — Robert of Lomene.

The King's Almswomen at Kington Priory.

Connected with the Priory, and perhaps forming part of it, was a dwelling for two pauper women, for whose maintenance the Prioress received annually six marks from the Crown. Of the origin of the charity there is no account. It may have been this Royal bounty that gave rise to the tradition mentioned above, of the Priory itself having been founded by the Empress Matilda. The House for the two paupers was built in 1221, (6 Hen. III.) as appears by a writ to the Treasurer of the Exchequer to pay 40s. "for the construction of one in the Priory of Kington for the use of the two Eleemosinary Damsels dwelling there during the King's pleasure." In the Close Rolls about this date, are orders for timber to be taken out of Chippenham Forest for this purpose; and also for payment of the six marks. And in 1223 a writ was issued to the Constable of Devizes (who was ex-officio Warden of Chippenham Forest) " commanding him that without delay, he do at once cause to be carried to Kinton for the use of the two Damsels residing there by the King's command, 20 cartloads of burl-wood " [Bruel, *copse*]. " And we much wonder that our precept heretofore sent by us relating unto this matter has not been carried into effect."

CHARTERS OF ST. MARY'S PRIORY.[1]

I. *Robert of Bryntone gives Tithes at Ewerne Stapleton, near Stourpayne, Co. Dorset.*

"To Jocelyn[2] Bishop of Sarum, and Adelelm Archdeacon of Dorset, Robert de Bryntone, greeting. I and Eva my wife, with Emma her sister, have granted the church of Iwerne for ever, and whatever else in the said church belongs to us, with all liberties &c., as Aluric the Priest held them: Witnesses, Richard the Canon: Robert de Huntsland: Richard son of Coloman: Robert of Acford: Wyger: Robert of the Gate: and the whole Halimote. Farewell."

II. *Confirmation of a grant of Lazarton,[3] or Lacerton near Stourpayne, Co. Dorset, which had been made to the Nuns by Robert de Brintone, Eva his wife, and Emma her sister, about 1142-1184.*

"Jocelyn, Bishop of Sarum, to Adelelm Archdeacon of Dorset: I confirm the grant of the Church of Lazarton, which Robert de Brinton, &c., gave to the Nuns of Kington; and because it is poor, I release it from all payments, except synodals. Witnesses, Humfrey the Canon: Walter the Canon: Dunecane the Chaplain."

III. *Adam (Weyfer) of Brimpton gives all his land at Kington St. Michael.*

"Omnibus, &c. To all the faithful in Christ, &c., Adam de Brinton greeting. Know that I have granted to God and St. Mary, and yᵉ Nuns of Kyngton, All the land in that vill which the s ᵈNuns hold of me, in pure and perpetual alms: free of all secular demands and services. And this I do for the good of my soul, and those of my Father and Mother, of my predecessors and successors. And I and my Heirs will warrant the same unto the said Nuns, free of all service to yᵉ Crown: specially that for ⅓ of the Knights Fee, wʰ they are wont to do unto me. Sealed with my seal. Witnesses, Richard, Canon of Sarum: Walter, Chaplain: H. Bigod: Robert de Brolett, Alexander his son, and Roger Poltemore; with many others.

---

[1] Translated from the Latin Deeds printed in the New Monasticon, (vol. iv. p. 398) and there described as having been taken (with the exception of No. II.) from the Priory Register, formerly in the possession of John Aubrey Esq., of Easton Piers.

[2] Bishop A.D. 1142.—1184.

[3] The Prioress of Kington presented twice to Lazarton, viz.: in 1339 and 1348. Afterwards the Bishop of Sarum "*jure devoluto.*" Lazarton Rectory, worth five marks per annum, being too poor to maintain its own Rector, was annexed to Stourpayne in 1431; the Prioress consenting to receive in lieu of her rights a pension of 6s. 8d. per annum. This pension, after the Dissolution, continued to be paid out of Stourpayne to the Long Family who had purchased all the Estate of Kington Priory. (See Hutchins, Dorset, I. 106, 107.)

IV. *Sir Hugh Mortimer,*[1] *Lord of the Fee, confirms No. III.*

"Hugh de Mortymer to all his Barons and Men, French and English, in England. Know that I have granted to God, St. Mary, and the Nuns of Kington serving God there, in pure and perpetual alms, for the salvation of my Soul, and that of my Father, my Mother, and Roger my Brother, All the land which Adam de Bryntone holds of my Fee in the same vill: he granting and confirming the same by Deed; which R. the son of Weyfer of Brintone gave to them when he founded the Place. To be free from all claims so far as concerns my Fee, &c. Witnesses, R. the Chaplain: R. de Brinton: Wm. Rudele: Aluric le Chamberlein: and others."

V. *Petronilla Bluet gives land at Bradley near Alton, Hants.*

"I Petronilla Bluet, wife of Wm. de Felcham give to God, St. Mary, and the Nuns of Kington, all my land in Bradley, to be held as I have held the same of Thomas son of Wm. de Salemonville, viz.: paying 5 shillings a year for all services, save that to the Crown for $\frac{1}{2}$ a Knight's fee. And because I bought that land of the said Thomas to be held by hereditary right, I make God and the Church of Kington St. Michael's and the Nuns my Heirs to hold the same of the said Thomas by the services aforesaid. Sealed with my seal. Witnesses, Ralph Bloet, Ralph his son; Ralph Bloet, son of Walter Bloet; Richard de Herierd, Robert Fitzpayn, Roger his son; Wm. Briwere, Peter de Scudamore, Rob. de Berkley, John de Warre, Helias de Stodeley, Gilbert, the Chaplain: Robert, Chaplain: Walter the Clerk, who drew this Deed: and others."

VI. *Richard de Heriet gives Tithes at Somerford,* (between A.D. 1194 and 1203.)

"Richard de Heriet in the presence of the Lord Herbert Bp. of Sarum, and of William of St. Mary's Church, Archdeacon of Wilts, gives to God and St. Mary and the Church of Kington and yᵉ Nuns there, the Church of Somerford; for the health of his soul: &c."[2]

VII. *Roger de Mortimer*[3] *gives Tythes at Stratfield Mortimer, &c.:* (before A.D. 1206.)

"Roger de Mortimer for the good of his soul and that of the Lady Isabella

---

[1] The Mortimers (*De Mortuo Mari*) a great Norman Family related to Wm. the First, naturally had large possessions assigned to them at the Conquest. Sir Hugh died 1227. His elder Brother Roger (ancestor of the Earls of March) in 1215. Their Mother was Matilda Longespeé.

[2] Herbert Prior Bp. of Sarum 1194—1217. William, Archdeacon of Wilts died about 1203. In Hen. III. "The Prioress of Kington held in Sum'ford $\frac{1}{4}$ᵈ of a Knight's Fee of Godfrey Sifrewast: He of the Earl of Sarum: He of the Crown." (*Test. de Nev.*)

[3] Roger Mortimer (grandfather of Sir Hugh and Roger, in Deed IV.) died 7 John (1206): having married for his second wife, Isabella, sister and heir of Hugh de Ferrars. Stratfield Mortimer is south of Reading: on the borders of Berks and Hants. By Biselee is probably meant *Riseley* in that neighbourhood.

his wife, for the souls of their Parents and successors, gives to God, St. Mary and the Nuns of Kington, &c., All the Tythe of Bread and Herrings of his house, of Biselee, of Stratfield and of Worthe.

"Witnesses, Philip de Mortimer, Wm. de Mortimer, Henry de Hillford, Ralph the Chaplain, Thomas, Clerk: Robert Corbet, Ernaldo de Bosco, Hankin de Camerâ, Ralph de Gueres, &c."

VIII. *Grant by Wm. Malreward, of the Church of Twerton.*[1]

"Know all present and future generations that I Wm. Malreward have given the Church of Twerton, free of all services to Kington Monastery and the Nuns: saving Episcopal rights. Witnesses, Thomas de Erlega, Archdeacon of Wells, Richard, Archdeacon of Bath: Ilbert, Precentor of Wells."

IX. *Confirmation of No. VIII., by Godfrey Malreward.*

"To all children of Holy Church, &c. Godfrey Malreward son of Godfrey M. greeting. Know that I have examined the grants of my great grandfather Wm. M., and of my grandfather Godfrey M. made to the Nuns of Kington, of the advowson of Twerton; and I confirm the same. Witnesses, John, Abbot of Keynsham, Master Henry de Cerne, &c."

X. *Grant of Alexander of Studley,* (about A.D. 1280.)

"A. de Studley gives, &c., the Grange which the Nuns have built in his Barton of Studley, and the site where the Grange is built: And in his Barton of Cadenham a place to build another Grange in, viz.: Between his Grange and Whitmere. Also he grants to the Nuns all his Tithes of Studley, Redmore, and Cadenham, to receive the same at the Door of his Grange, and to have a Store at his Mill to deposit the same. Witnessed by John de St. Quintin, Henry de Cerne, Adam Delamere, Thos. Burell, Henry Kaynel."[2]

XI. *R. Burnell, Bishop of Bath and Wells, gives an acre of land at Kington; and the Rectory.*

19 Edw. I. (1290.) "Robert Burnell, Bishop of Bath and Wells, grants to God and the Church of St. Mary of the Nuns, and to Claricia Prioress, in free alms, one acre of land in Kington St. Michael in the East Field, in the ploughed ground called 'Goldshawe,' between the land of the Prioress on the East, and land of Richard Carpenter on the West, with the Advowson of the Church.

---

[1] The Church of Twerton, near Bath, was valued in 1318 at 6 marks; a vicarage was ordained in 1342. The Vicar to pay to the Prioress 100 shillings yearly: and as often as he should fail, to forfeit one mark to the building of Bath Abbey. (Wells Reg. and Coll. Som. iii. 348.) In the Priory "Book of Obits," Reginald (Fitz Jocelyn, 1174) is named as the donor of Twerton Parsonage: and in Harl. MS. 6964, p. 22, the Rectory is stated to have been appropriated to the Nuns 12 May 1322.

[2] The concurrence of witnesses to this Deed is curious; showing the origin of the names of the five Parishes, Stanton *St. Quintin*, Draycote *Cerne*, Leigh-*Delamere*, Langley *Burell*, and Yatton *Kaynell*.

Witnesses, John Delamere, Godfrey de Wrokeshale, Henry de Cerne, John Mauduit Knight, Richard Pigot, Roger de Cumb, Reginald Croke, and others."[1]

XII. *Wm. Harptree of Harptree, Co. Som. grants Tithes at Stourpayne, Co. Dorset.*

"Wm. son of John of Harptree, with consent of Matilda his wife and their heirs, grants to the Nuns the Tythes of Corn in Stures and Sanford, and the Tenth of 'meat not bought' there." (Quære, of stock bred and killed by himself?) "Witnesses, Richard Abbot of Keynsham, Wm. Abbot of Kingswood, &c."[2]

XIII. *Grant of Roger de Villiers, at Stourpayne.*[3]

"Roger de Villiers gives the second Tythes of his demesne lands at Stures and Sanford, and 10th of 'meat not bought': respecting which a Plea was moved between him and the Nuns before commissioners appointed by the Apostolic See, viz.: Albert, Prior of Brhuperia[4] and Dean of Christianity of the same Province: To hold the same, in as full manner as they had been given by his uncle Richard, son of Elias de Orescueil, to the said Nuns. Sealed, &c."

THE PRIORY AFTER THE DISSOLUTION.

At the Dissolution the whole Priory Estate, including Kington Rectory, was granted (30 June 1538), to Sir Richard Long, younger brother of Sir Henry Long of Draycote who had been its chief Seneschal.[5] The Rectorial Tithe of Kington continues now to be part of the property of that family, represented by Viscount Wellesley. The House and lands about it were afterwards sold in 1556 to John Taylor of Castle Combe.[6] Isaac Taylor (brother of John, Vicar of Kington) resided there in 1570. His daughter

---

[1] This Deed (printed also twice in the old Edition of the Monasticon, I. 534 and II. 889.) is the first in which the name of Kington *St. Michael* appears to be found.

[2] See Valor Eccl. I. 269. The Harptrees of East Harptree, Co. Som. (under which manor Stourpayne in Dorset was held), afterwards took the name of Gournay. Coll. Som. iii. 587.

[3] See Hutch. Dor. I. 107. There is no mention, in the Val. Eccl., of this as belonging to Kington Priory.

[4] Probably meant for Beaurepaire (*vulgò* Baruper), near Basingstoke.

[5] Rot. xxx. 30. Hen. VIII. But by an Inquisition at Warminster 19 Dec. 3 and 4 Phil. and Mary (1556-7), on the death of Henry Long of Draycote, (elder brother of the grantee), it was found that the said *Henry* held the Rectory of Kington St. Michael, by the 20th part of a Knight's fee under the King: and that Robert was his son and heir. (Harl. MS. 757. f. 243.)

[6] Rot. cxiij. 3 and 4 Phil. and Mary.

Eleanor married Thomas Lyte of Easton Piers, and was great grandmother to John Aubrey. In 1628 it was sold by John Taylor to Thomas Tyndale Esq., (then late of Eastwood Park near Thornbury), and Dorothy (Stafford) his wife. Mr. and Mrs. Tyndale lived here and were buried at Kington Church.[1] In 1677 Mr. Thomas Tyndale third son of the purchaser, sold the Priory to Mr. Richard Sherwin, who had bought Aubrey's Estate at Lower Easton Piers a few years before. In the middle of the last century the Priory belonged to the family of Hale of Locksley, Co. Herts.; and in 1796, at the sale of Mr. Wm. Hale's Wiltshire Estates it was bought by the present owner, Mr. Sutton.

The Chartulary or Register Book of this Priory is missing. In 1620 it was in the possession of Sir Wm. Pole.[2] Sir Robert Long had it in Aubrey's time 1670.[3] Tanner refers to Sir Robert's volume as in the hands, first of John Aubrey, then 1695 of his brother William, and afterwards, of Mr. Rogers of Chippenham.

EASTON PIERS, OR PERCY.

This is a small hamlet of four detached farms, forming the North-western division of the Parish of Kington St. Michael. The tything is not in the Hundred of North Damerham, but of Malmsbury; the reason of which is, that Easton Percy was not held under the Abbey of Glastonbury. The principal house is the "Manor Farm." The others are "Upper Easton Percy," a little further west. Beyond that and nearer Yatton Keynell, "Cromwells": and on the southern slope below the Manor House, and nearest to Kington, "Lower Easton Percy."

The Tything occupies a well wooded grassy ridge, running east and west between Kington St. Michael and Yatton Kaynell: parallel with the Parish of Leigh Delamere on the north. The soil is chiefly such as belongs to the siliceous sandstones of the Forest Marble, yielding healthy dry pasture. It is on as high ground as

---

[1] An elaborate Pedigree of this Family was privately printed by their descendant the late George Booth Tyndale Esq., of Lincoln's Inn Fields.

[2] Collect. Top. et Gen. I. 207.

[3] Note on back of Title page of Aubrey's original MS. Coll. for N. Wilts Ashm. Mus.

any in the neighbourhood : and is traversed through its full length by a very narrow winding lane crossed by gates, and overshadowed by steep banks and old picturesque trees.   Aubrey speaks of "other old ways now lost, but some vestiges left:" amongst them, "a way by the Pound and the Manor House leading northwards to Leigh Delamere, and southwards to Allington ; but of that no sign left." This however, for some part of the distance northwards, still continues to be used as a bridle path through the fields ; and at each end, both under Easton Manor House, and at Leigh Delamere, traces of the lane are distinct.

Easton Percy appears to have stood in ancient times, on the margin of a large unenclosed district.   "It butted upon Cotswold,[1] which is a ploughed campania : and mem : that fourscore years ago" (which would be about A.D. 1590,) "from Yatton Kaynell town's end to the Parson's close adjoining Easton Grounds all was common : and Yatton and Easton did intercommon, and put in cattle equally.   Between the two parishes of Easton Piers and Castle Combe much hath been enclosed in my remembrance, and every day more and more,[2] so also, between Kington St. Michael and Dracot Cerne all was common field : and the west field of Kington, between Easton Piers and Haywood, was enclosed in 1664.   The North part of Wilts was in those days admirable for field sports :" a species of celebrity which it still retains ; enclosures, stiff fences and gates, to the contrary nothing withstanding.

Easton Percy had once a Chapel, a grave yard, and village cross. The Chapel was taken down about A.D. 1610.   "It was but small :[3] and had a Turret for two Tintinnabula as at Leigh Delamere, Cerston and Brokenborough.   The toft where it stood is still called "Chapel-hay," near to the Mannor House.   They did bury here." (*Aubrey.*) "Chapel-land" is still the name of a ground about 100 yards N.W. of the Manor House.   At the upper end of it, an unevenness of surface marks the site of the building ; and in digging holes for planting, human bones are occasionally found.

---

[1] Aubrey.   The district now so called is many miles distant from Easton.
[2] Nat. Hist. of Wilts, p. 104.
[3] And so its perquisites.   "A.D. 1446. Allowance to the Clerk for stipend, 4d."

The name of one of the Incumbents appears in the Sarum Registry. In 1319 "John de Gyvleton" (no doubt, for "Yeovilton" the Family to whom, as will be seen, the Estate then belonged,) was presented to the Chapel of Easton Piers by Ralph de Cromhale Patron.[1] "The Font Stone was serving" (in Aubrey's time,) "at 'Cromwells' for cattle to drink."

The Cross stood at "the crosse way by the Pound, at the entrance into the Lane which heretofore went to Lye Delamere, close to the Mannour House."

MANORIAL HISTORY.

In the Reign of King Edward the Confessor, the Saxon owner was one Osward. At the Conquest it was part of the fee of Drogo de Fitz Ponz, of Seagry and Alderton, and was held under him by Gislebert. In Hen. III. Walter de Clifford held it under the Crown: Patrick Chaworth under him: under Chaworth, Henry Kaignel, and Philip de Lye; the latter by grand serjeanty of being the King's bowbearer. John of Eston, had ¼ of a Knight's fee. The Tything bore the name of Easton only until its connexion with the family of Piers, now commonly spelled Percy;[2] which addition appears to have been made about A.D. 1250.

To John Aubrey's partiality for his native nook of Wiltshire ground, we are indebted for the means of ascertaining its history at this period. His undigested "Collections for North Wilts" contain a number of ancient Latin documents relating to it, taken from the Title deeds of the farm, then his own. These occupy sixteen pages in Sir Thomas Phillipps's printed copy, pp. 69-85. Many of them being without date and all without arrangement, the labyrinth is not easily unravelled; but the substance seems to be this.

The proprietor about the year above mentioned, 1250, was Piers, or Fitz-piers: using more frequently, after the fashion of the times, a sirname from the property, De Eston. The first is Sir John, who gave to the Nuns of Kington a coppice and other ground

[1] Wilts Instit. p. 17.

[2] That *Piers* and *Percy*, if not one and the same name, were similarly pronounced, would appear from Falstaff's quibble; "Well, if Percy be alive, I'll pierce him." 1. Hen. IV., A. 5. Sc. 3.

between Easton and the Priory.   John, his son, was succeeded by
Sir Peter de Eston: he, by his daughter Joan, mentioned as Lady
of the Manor in 1332: Edmund de Easton, clerk, occurs in 1345,
(the seal to his Deed dated at Oxford, bearing a cross engrailed,
with an illegible inscription); and Walter Eston in 1483.   In
the Kalendar of Obits kept at St. Mary's Priory (printed above),
several benefactors of this family are registered: as, January 17,
Mary late Lady of Eston; May 7, Dame Johan of Eston, and
others.   Who they were might have been discovered in a MS.
volume (had it been forthcoming), referred to by Aubrey, "The
Leiger Book of Tropenell at Col. Wm. Eyre's at Neston: where
mention is made of Pierse and his coat, azure 5 milpecks or fusils.
This MS." he adds " is the best key to open the knowledge of the
old and lost families, which is my search."[1]

Piers was succeeded by De Yeovilton of Somersetshire.   In a
Deed of about 1300, Wm. Seward of Easton grants his tenements,
&c., to John de Yeovilton and Joan his wife: and in 1306 the
Manor suffered a recovery to Philip de Paunton[2] and his wife, who
was probably of the Yeovilton family.   In 1361 Peter de Yeovilton
being about to go into foreign parts, conveys his Estate at Eston,
with Speckington and others in Somersetshire and Devon, to
Nicholas de Yeovilton and Richard his son, upon condition that if
he returns home safe, he is to have possession again.   In 1396 Sir
Robert de Yeovilton was owner of Easton.[3]   Margaret, heiress of
the family, married Thomas Pain of Painshay, Co. Devon.   Katharine Pain married John Sturton of Preston, and their daughter
Alice Sturton was wife of William Daubeney (ancestor of Henry
Earl of Bridgewater).   The estate thus came to his son Sir Giles,

[1] Coll. for N. Wilts, p. 68.

[2] Of Dorsetshire.   In 1299 Philip Paunton was of Charborough.   In 1337
Juliana Paunton; the reversion to Nicholas de Ivelton (Yeovilton).   In 1389
Richard Yeovilton.   (Hutchins. II. 184. 186.)

[3] Probably the Easton Knight, of whom an exploit is preserved in the parish
annals of Castle Combe. (Mr. P. Scrope's Hist., p. 249.) "Roger Young, junior,
dwelt in Castle Combe as a clothier in the time of King Edw. III., and a certain
Knight, Sir Robert Yevolton, in the time of K. Rich. II., came by force of arms
to beat Robert Young then dwelling in C. Combe: and the said Knight fled into
the Church of that place for safety of his body."

afterwards Lord Daubeney of Petherton, Co. Som., and his wife Elizabeth (Arundel). Having been one of the opponents to the designs of Richard Duke of Gloucester, Lord Daubeney was deprived of his lands, and in 1483 (1 Richard III.) Easton was granted to Ralph Willoughby, but was afterwards restored. Lord Daubeney before his death in 1507, sold it to Thomas Essex; in whose family it remained about 57 years.

The Pedigree and Arms of Essex are given by Aubrey (Coll. I. 86) as follows :

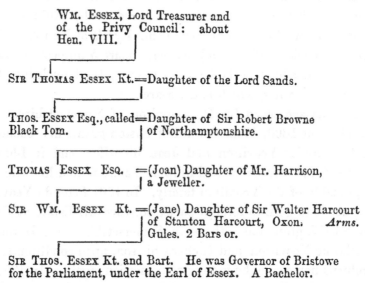

WM. ESSEX, Lord Treasurer and of the Privy Council: about Hen. VIII.

SIR THOMAS ESSEX Kt.==Daughter of the Lord Sands.

THOS. ESSEX Esq., called==Daughter of Sir Robert Browne Black Tom. | of Northamptonshire.

THOMAS ESSEX ESQ. ==(Joan) Daughter of Mr. Harrison, | a Jeweller.

SIR WM. ESSEX Kt. ==(Jane) Daughter of Sir Walter Harcourt | of Stanton Harcourt, Oxon. *Arms.* | Gules. 2 Bars or.

SIR THOS. ESSEX Kt. and Bart. He was Governor of Bristowe for the Parliament, under the Earl of Essex. A Bachelor.

Arms. 1. Azure a chevron engrailed ermine between 3 eagles displayed argent. (ESSEX.) 2. Sable, a chevron argent between 3 crescents ermine. 3. Gules, a fleur de lys argent. 4. Per fess dancetteè argent and gules. 5. Ermine.[1]

In 1564 Edward Essex and Anne his wife sold Easton to Sir Robert Sackville, Chancellor of the Court of Augmentations in the reign of Hen. VIII. Sir Robert Sackville the purchaser, was the father of Thomas Sackville Lord Buckhurst, first Earl of Dorset, a statesman and poet in the reigns of Queen Elizabeth and King

---

[1] Aubrey gives no authority for the Pedigree and Arms above described. The Arms do not correspond with those assigned to Essex of Bewcot in Berks, [*Extinct Bart.*] but the Pedigree is nearly the same.
Chap. House Fines.

James I. In Nov. 1574, Lord Buckhurst sold Easton to John and Thomas Lyte, then tenants under lease: and in January 1575, they sold the Manor House and Farm to John Snell Esq., father of Sir Thomas, of Kington St. Michael's. After an interval of 48 years Sir Charles Snell, son of Sir Thomas, in the year 1623 sold[1] the Manor Farm and House to John Langton of Bristol, merchant, in whose family it remained until the year 1704. A Pedigree of the Langtons, deduced chiefly from the Title Deeds, is annexed.

On the 28th March 1704, the Manor was again sold, (with lands in Kington and Yatton,) by Robert Langton and Anna his wife, to Walter White Esq., of Grittleton, for £3325: on whose death without issue in 1705 it passed, by marriage of his youngest sister and coheiress Elizabeth, to Richard Salwey Esq., of the Moor, Co. Salop. He died in 1712. In 1796 this Estate, the Priory of Kington and the Down Farm, all being then the property of Wm. Hale Esq., were sold by auction, when the Manor Farm was bought by Mr. Collett, then tenant, whose son is the present owner and occupier.

The Manor House is very large and well built, in the old Wiltshire style so common in this neighbourhood, with bold gables, ornamented freestone chimneys, and casement windows. In 1630, soon after it had passed from the Snells to the Langtons, all the older house then standing was taken down and rebuilt, except the Hall and some smaller portions. The parts rebuilt by the Langtons are distinguished by dates and initials. On one chimney " I L. A L. 1630." (John and Alice Langton): on another "T L. 1664." (Thomas Langton): and on the west front "I L. 1631." (John Langton). The older part which they did not take down, is still left, and forms a north wing. Its principal window, described by Aubrey as of " peculiar old fashion," is of six lights, divided by stone mullions and crossed by one transom. Above it is another, once of like size, but now partly blocked up. The two stand out in bold projection under a sloping tiled roof. The other windows in this more ancient portion, being of ecclesiastical style with cinquefoil

---

[1] Sir Charles's reason for selling is mentioned above p. 45. The succeeding links in the history are taken from the original documents in the author's possession.

PEDIGREE OF LANGTON OF EASTON PERCY, WILTS.

[From the Title Deeds, and Thos. Gore's MSS.]

Arms. Quarterly, or and gules, a bend sable.

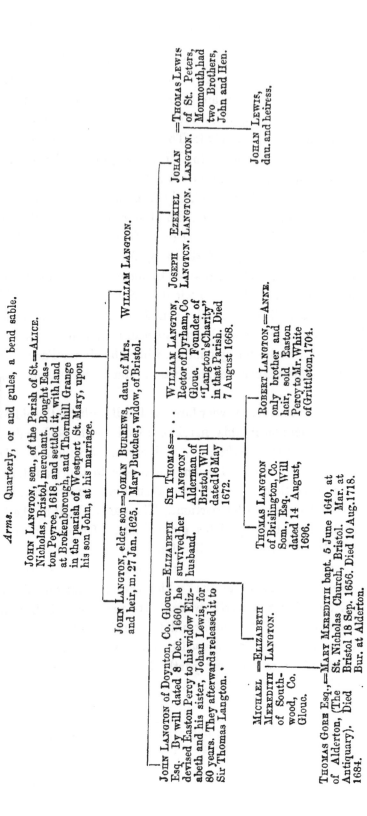

JOHN LANGTON, sen., of the Parish of St.==ALICE.
Nicholas, Bristol, merchant. Bought Easton Peyrce, 1618, and settled it, with land
at Brokenborough, and Thornhill Grange
in the parish of Westport St. Mary, upon
his son John, at his marriage.

WILLIAM LANGTON.

JOHN LANGTON, elder son==JOHAN BURREWS, dau. of Mrs.
and heir, m. 27 Jan. 1825. | Mary Butcher, widow, of Bristol.

SIR THOMAS==..
LANGTON,
Alderman of
Bristol. Will
dated 16 May
1672.

WILLIAM LANGTON,
Rector of Dyrham, Co
Glouc. Founder of
"Langton's Charity"
in that Parish. Died
7 August 1668.

JOSEPH
LANGTCN.

EZEKIEL
LANGTON.

JOHAN
LANGTON. ==THOMAS LEWIS
of St. Peters,
Monmouth, had
two Brothers,
John and Hen.

JOHN LANGTON of Doynton, Co. Glouc.==ELIZABETH
Esq. By will dated 8 Dec. 1660, he | survived her
devised Easton Percy to his widow Eliz- | husband.
abeth and his sister, Johan Lewis, for
80 years. They afterwards released it to
Sir Thomas Langton. '

THOMAS LANGTON
of Brislington, Co.
Som., Esq. Will
dated 14 August,
1696.

ROBERT LANGTON,==ANNE.
only brother and
heir, sold Easton
Percy to Mr. White
of Grittleton, 1704.

JOHAN LEWIS,
dau. and heiress.

MICHAEL ==ELIZABETH
MEREDITH | LANGTON.
of South-
wood, Co.
Glouc.

THOMAS GORE Esq.,==MARY MEREDITH bapt. 5 June 1640, at
of Alderton, (The | St. Nicholas Church, Bristol. Mar. at
Antiquary). Died | Bristol 18 Sep. 1656. Died 10 Aug. 1718.
1684. | Bur. at Alderton.

EASTON PERCY MANOR HOUSE.
(NORTH FRONT.)

REV. J. E. JACKSON, DEL.   EDW. KITE. LITH.

heads, and its angles being flanked by bold buttresses with a sub-
stantial moulding running all round, about a yard from the
ground, the wing looks not unlike a chapel; but it was the original
hall. The room is paved with freestone, in lozenge. It was once
wainscotted with carved oak panel: and a few relics of better days,
such as stag's antlers, &c., still linger on the walls, as if to declare
that it was not always filled with piles of sacks, cider-presses, and
other farm house gear, as it is now. The whole house indeed, is one
of the many warnings which every county, not omitting Wiltshire,
presents, of the "base uses" that await a goodly residence. For
such is its loneliness and perilous state of dilapidation, that it seems
to want but one thing more, which is, to be fixed upon as the scene
of a tragical legend or ghost story. It is very little known, and if
any reader, on mysterious fiction bent, will select a gloomy day, or
visit it at nightfall, he will be grateful for the suggestion. Yet the
situation is one of the best in the neighbourhood, and the views
(did the dense screen of trees permit any) extensive; northward
over Stanton Park and Leigh Delamere; on the south, across a
prettily wooded lawn to Lower Easton in the foreground, and the
Calne Hills in the distance. Aubrey mentions that "Herons bred
here in 1580 before the great oaks were felled down near the
Manor House."

LOWER EASTON PERCY.

When Thomas Lyte sold the Manor in 1575 to Mr. Snell, he
retained part of it, and built a house on the brow of the hill above
the brook, facing south east.[1] In that house (afterwards destroyed)
John Aubrey was born.[2] He was of the younger branch of the
Aubreys of Llantrithyd in Glamorganshire, but his father Richard,
of Broad Chalk in South Wilts, having married Deborah grand-
daughter of Thomas Lyte of Easton Piers, John Aubrey succeeded
to this Farm as his mother's inheritance. The Lytes were brought
hither from Somersetshire by the Yeoviltons, and may have been

---

[1] The sloping ground in front now called "Bounds" formerly "Brown's Hill,"
is mentioned by Aubrey as opposite the house in which he was born. (N. H. of
Wilts, p. 49.)

[2] A memoir of him will be found in a later page.

related to them.   The village of Lyte's Cary in that county, named
after the family, is close to Yeovilton and Speckington.   The account
given by Aubrey of his mother's family, is, that they held Easton
Piers either in lease or by inheritance 249 years; "from Henry VI.
The father of Thos. Lyte who purchased, had £800 per ann. in
Leases: viz., all Easton, except Cromwell's farm, (£20): and also
the farm of Didmarton and Sopworth."

Of his home Aubrey has preserved a sketch in one of his MSS.
in the Ashmolean Museum, Oxford.[1]   "From the garret a delicate

Lower Easton Piers.   The birth-place of John Aubrey, (*destroyed.*)

prospect.   The garden was laid out in the Italian style, upon three
different levels, each raised upon the other, and ascended by flights
of steps with a *jet d'eau* in the lowest.   About it were groups of
trees, a pillar and volant Mercury, &c., &c."   The ground still
retains some marks of this arrangement.   In a bedroom on a chimney were two escutcheons.   1. Arms of Lyte, (see Pedigree;) over
this "Isaac Lyte" (Aubrey's grandfather) "Natus 1576" (the

---

[1] The name of this MS. is "Easton Piers delineated: or Designatio de E.P.
in com. Wilts, per me [heu] infortunatum J. A., Reg. Soc. Socium. A.D. 1669."
It consists of 19 oblong quarto leaves, with outline views of the house, gardens,
and environs of Easton Piers; from one of which the wood cut is copied.   The
old House seems to have been altered (perhaps by Aubrey himself) into an
Italian Villa, of which he has also preserved a sketch.   Mr. Britton remembered
a ruinous dwelling here, the windows and doors taken away, walls covered with
ivy, floors fallen in and much decayed, the whole shut in, as it is now, by
orchards and gardens.

PEDIGREE OF LYTE OF EASTON PERCY.

Arms. Gules; a chevron between 3 swans argent: a mullet sable for difference.

RICHARD LYTE=JOAN GALE of
of Lyte's Cary, | Sutton Benger,
and of Didmar- | bur. at K. St.
ton. (Wilts Vis. | M. 1563.
1623.)

JOHN LYTE mar.=ELEANOR
July 1567. (P.R.) | Power of
Sold Upper Eas- | Stanton
ton Piers 1571. | Farm.

THOMAS LYTE sold=ELEANOR, (first wife) d. of=ELIZABETH,
E.P. Manor Farm | Isaac Taylor | of the Priory, | (second wife)
1574: and built | mar. 1508. | Died 1582. | Bur. at Kin.
Lower E.P. Bur. | (Wilts Vis.) | | 1597.
1627, æt 96.

ALICE=JOHN
| LYTE, DEEKE.
| marr.
| 1576.
| P.R.

JOHN LYTE NICHOLAS=
bap. 1569. LYTE bap.
1573.P.R.

MARY b. 1568.
SARAH b. 1571.

ISAAC LYTE=ISRAEL
bap. 1576. | BROWNE.
Bur.25Feb.
1659.

JOHN
bur.
1659.

ANNE, JANE, SIMON,
b. 1571. b. 1579. b. 1582.
bur.1584.

MARGARET, ELEANOR,
bur. 1570. bur. 1575.

RICHARD AUBREY=DEBORAH LYTE,
Esq. of Burleton, | sole d. and h. m.
Co. Hereford, and | at K. 15 June
Broad Chalk, | 1625.bur.25 Ap.
Wilts. Bur. at K. | 1686. P.R.
1652.

THOMAS. WILLIAM,
d.Oct.1707.

ANNE, ISAAC bur. 1629.
1628. ISAAC bur. 1632.

ISAAC LYTE bap. 26 Dec. 1612.=
Alderman of London. *Founder*
of the Almshouses at Kington.
Will dated 15Feb. 1672. Prov.
21 Aug. 1673 in P.C. of C.

BENJAMIN, MARY, b. 1610.
(Twin with ANNE, b. 1604.
Isaac) died SARAH, b. 1606.
inf.

FRANCIS =ELIZABETH.
GOODENOUGH.

JOHN AUBREY Esq, the Antiquary,
born at Lower Easton, bap. at K. 12
March 1625-6.

same year in which the house was built). 2. Arms of Browne of Winterbourne Basset. An eagle displayed sable, legged gules: on its breast a crescent or. Over this, "Israel Lyte" [his grandmother.]

Lower Easton Piers was sold by Aubrey in his day of adversity to Mr. Richard Sherwin.[1] In 1796 it formed part of Mr. Hale's property (mentioned above, p. 77.) and was sold in 1796 to Mr. Skeate, whose representatives are now the proprietors.

UPPER EASTON PIERS.

This is a small farmhouse with about 98 acres attached, lying westwards of the Manor House, between it and "Cromwell's." It was severed from the principal estate in 1574 by sale from John and Thomas Light of Easton Piers, to Nicholas Light of Leigh Delamere. About a century afterwards it belonged to Mr. Benjamin Hinde, an attorney, steward to Sir Charles Snell, and son of Richard Hinde, Vicar of Kington St. Michael. It has continued in this family about 300 years, being now the property of the Rev. Thomas Lowe, Vicar of Willington, Sussex, in right of his mother, Susannah coheiress of the late Thomas Hinde, D.D., Rector of Ardeley near Bicester. The Doctor's great grandfather was the Rev. Richard Hinde, Rector of Grittleton.

CROMHALE'S.

Commonly called Cromwell's, is a small tenement of 30 acres with a house, bounding on Yatton Keynell, and takes its name from ancient owners. Ralph de Cromhale, Chaplain, has been already mentioned as Patron of Easton Chapel in 1319. It seems never to have been part of the principal manor.

A small holding adjoining Cromhale's (now Mr. Butler's) belonged in 1300 to the estate of the Keynell family, from which the parish of Yatton takes its name.

THE VICARAGE.

Two names only remain of the period during which Kington had its Clerical Rector resident, appointed by the Abbot of Glastonbury;

---

[1] On the back of the MS. account of his Villa, Aubrey has written, "Nunc mea, mox hujus, sed postea nescio cujus."

viz.: William St. Faith *(de Sanctâ Fide)* for 50 years from c. 1173; and Jordan Cotel.[1] Soon after that time the Tithes were appropriated, and a vicarage ordained. The advowson (as before stated), was awarded after the Glastonbury quarrel to the Bishop of Wells, who gave the Tithe of the Rectory and right of presentation to the vicarage, to the Prioress of St. Mary's. In temp. Hen. VIII., both were purchased by the Longs of Draycote, to whose representative, Viscount Wellesley, they now belong.

Amongst former Vicars of whom any thing more is known than their mere names, were, 1612—1663, Richard Hind[2] of Ch. Ch. Oxon, afterwards Rector of Boddington, Co. Northamp., and of Grittleton, where he was also Patron. Benjamin Griffin, 1712—16, who built vicarage houses here and at Colerne. William Harington, of the Kelston family (near Bath), vicar 34 years, died 1751. From 1751—77, John Scrope D.D., also Rector of Castle Combe, and for three years before his death owner of that estate: a scholar, and author of some works on divinity.[3] From 1779—1824, Edmund Garden; died in his 93rd year, having been nearly 60 years Reader to Gray's Inn. To the present Incumbent, the Rev. Edward Charles Awdry, appointed in 1856, the Parish is already indebted for his prompt determination to restore

The Church of St. Michael.

How and when it obtained this name has been mentioned, p. 39. It consists of a Chancel, Nave with north and south aisles, a Tower at the west end, and south Porch, *(see plates.)* The Chancel arch is of the 12th century; and one of its windows is enriched with Early English Tooth-moulding, very delicately worked. The east

---

[1] "Cotel had some estate in Kington Parish; according to the Legier of Tropnell: and beareth gules, bend or."—(Aubrey.)

[2] Thus mentioned by Aubrey. "Mr. Thos. Hobbes told me, that Col. Charles Cavendish who had travelled over Greece, told him that the Greeks doe sing their Greek. In Herefordshire they have a touch of this singing. Our old divines had. Our old vicar of Kington St. Michael, Mr. Hynd, did *sing* his sermons rather than reade them. You may find in Erasmus that the monks used this fashion, who mocks them, that sometimes they would be very low, and by and by they would be mighty high, *quando nihil opus est.*" (Aubrey's Lives. vol. ii. p. 274.)

[3] History of Castle Combe. p. 352.

window was of temp. Hen. VI., and formerly (in Aubrey's time) contained three figures in stained glass, bearing the names of Thomas Nye[1] ("in the habit of a lawyer like Judge Littleton at Worcester"): his wife Margaret, and Christine Nye. The latter was Prioress of Kington and probably gave the window. The one next to it, on the south side, contained the figure of another Prioress, Lady Cicely Bodenham. The Nave arches are Early English; and some aisle windows once had slender marble shafts of that date. In the south aisle, where the east window is Decorated, are the usual signs of a private altar.[2] The north aisle was cheaply rebuilt in 1755, when an old Norman door was destroyed. Against the angle of the Chancel outside is the projection commonly called a "Lychnoscope." The original Porch, long since destroyed, had a head over the doorway, called by tradition King Ethelred's: whose figure, with that of his Queen, was once on a window of the south aisle. Of these Aubrey has preserved drawings. The present inner door has Norman shafts, surmounted by a flat-headed arch of the 15th century. The tower, formerly Norman and supporting a spire, was in great peril of falling when Aubrey made his sketch, showing large cracks in the walls. Referring to the previous case of Calne steeple in 1645, he predicted a similar catastrophe here. "Such will be the fate of our's at Kington: one cannot persuade the Parishioners to go out of their own way."[3] And so it came to pass. The parishioners went on in their own way, the gaping walls in theirs; till the great storm of 1703 put an end to the discussion by blowing the whole down. The tower was rebuilt, but in meagre style and without spire, in 1725.

On one of the original bells had been the legend " ✝. *Sancte Michael ora pro nobis.*" Another ("a daintie little one") was stolen in 1649. The present peal of six was cast by Abraham Rudhall in 1726. The first rings out "Prosperity to the Parish"; the

---

[1] A Herman Nye was Rector of Crudwell in N. Wilts, 1445.

[2] On the cieling of the South Aisle, formerly painted and gilt in panels, were remaining c. 1670, on shields; 1, A saltire cross, 2. The Pope's arms, 2 keys in saltire and a cross in pale. 3. Azure, a stag at gaze or. 4. A Portcullis or. 5. A Marshal's bolt, or fetterlock.

[3] Nat. Hist. of Wilts, p. 99.

second "Peace and good neighbourhood"; the third "Prosperity to the Church of England"; the fourth "Wm. Harington, vicar". Fifth, the date only. Sixth, "Jonathan Power and Robert Hewitt, Ch-wardens."

One Adam Milsham "an old wealthy bachelor, and a native of Kington," invested part of his wealth in the year 1639 in the purchase of a Clock and Chimes: and by his will left £10 more to be applied to the repair of the latter. But in the meanwhile a smith, being parish clerk " in the troublesome days," converted the iron of the musical accompaniment to his own use. So, in 1708, the Parish did the same with the Legacy.

The present silver chalice bears the date of 1571, and is probably the one given by Nicholas Snell Esq., but it has lost the family crest, (a demi-talbot) originally on the cover. Mrs. Harington (the vicar's wife) gave in 1755 a silver paten.

The Registers commence Oct. 6, 1563, John Tayler, vicar. The entries for 1663 appear to be missing, but otherwise the volumes are fairly preserved. In 1582 is this memorandum, " Here the Plague began 4 May," and " 6 August. Here the Plague rested." Out of eighteen persons who died of it, eight were of one family, named Kington, John Aubrey's tenants at Lower Easton Percy. The entries of his Parents' burials are in Aubrey's own writing.

MONUMENTS.

Many have been removed or destroyed during alterations: but of their names and some of their inscriptions Aubrey has left copies. In the Chancel, near the middle, were

A.D. 1577. The Right Worshipfull NICHOLAS SNELL Esq.
　　　1612. SIR THOMAS SNELL.
　　　1651. "Here underneath this stone lieth interred the bodie of SIR CHARLES SNELL Knight who deceased the 24th day of November in the yeare of Lord 1651 aged 61."

Against the east wall there is an old painting of the Arms of this family. *Quarterly,* 1 *and* 4. *Gules and azure, over all a cross flory or :* SNELL. 2 *and* 3. *Sable, on a fess or between six arrows three blackamoors' heads.* KEYNELL. (This is the coat given to Keynell by Aubrey, and it is on the stone screen in Yatton Keynell

Church. The Heralds give a different one.) Below was once written
" *In memoriam Caroli Snell Militis, qui obiit Nov. 24. 1651.*" The words
" *In cruce victoria* " are still left.

Next to the above interment :

Arms. *On a lozenge, barry of 6 gules and argent, a chief or.*
Englefield. Impaling, *Sable, on a bend cotised 3 lions passant.*
Browne.

" Here under this stone lyeth the bodie of the late Dame Jane Englefield,
widowe of Sir Francis Englefield Bart., deceased: eldest daughter of Anthony
Browne Esq. eldest son to Henry Lord Viscount Mountague of Cowdray in the
Countie of Sussex. She departed this life the 17th September 1650 aged 75
years. Of your charitie say one Ave and a Pater-noster."

The last line is remarkable in a *Church* so late as 1650. This
Lady was of Fasterne near Wotton Basset. One of her grand-
daughters married a Thomas Stokes Esq., (a name connected with
this Parish,) which may account for her interment here. (see Extinct Barts. "Englefield.")

In S.E. corner. 1652. (John Aubrey's Father.)

" Hic jacet quod reliquum est Richardi Awbrey Armigeri, qui obiit 22 die
mensis Octobris, MDCLII."

It was Aubrey's intention to erect a little tablet of white marble
" about an ell high or better," to both his parents, but this was
never done. The inscription prepared by him was as follows :—

" P.M. Richardi Awbrey Armig. filii unici Johannis Awbrey de Burlton
in Agro Heref.: filii tertii Gulielmi Awbrey L.L.D^ris et e Supplicum libellis
Eliz. Reg. Mag^ri viri pacifici et fidelis amici. Uxorem duxit Deborah Filiam
et hæredem Isaaci Lyte de Easton Piers, per quam suscepit tres superstites
Johannem, Gulielmum, et Thomam, filios. Obiit xxi° die Octr. A.D. 1652.
Ætat: 49."

Of his father Aubrey adds that " Alexander Brome hath an
Elegie on him in his poems, (his Christian name having been
omitted); which he made at the request of his next neighbour and
friend Mr. Isaac Lyte late Alderman of London, my kinsman:"
(and Founder of the Almshouses at Kington). At the time of
writing this Epitaph his mother was living, as he adds, " I would
have a blank of two lines for my mother." He has also left on a
scrap of paper lying amongst his MSS. at Oxford, an inscription for
a monument to himself, from which, as he did not die until 1697,
it would seem that he expected an earlier death. The memorandum
consists of a shield, bearing six quarterings, " Aubrey, Einon,

Morgan, Danvers, Blount of Mangotsfield, and Lyte : or else thus,. Aubrey, Danvers, Blount, and Lyte." "Consule Mr. A. W. de hiis." *(Ask Mr. Antony Wood about these.)*

"Heic situs est, Johannes Awbrey, Filius et hæres Rich. Awbrey de Easton Piers in Agro Wilt. armig: Reg. Soc; Socii. Obiit Aº Dni 168 . . . Die mensis . . . Aº Ætatis suæ 6 . . ."

At west end of Chancel,

1664. Arms. *Argent, on a fess gules between 3 garbs sable. a martlet of the first :* Tyndale. Impaling, *Or, a chevron gules. charged with a crescent ; a canton ermine.* Stafford.

"Here lyeth the body of Dorothy late wife of Mr. Thos. Tyndale and. daughter of William Stafford Esqʳ : who departed this Life 20 July 1664 aged near 72."

"Here lieth the body of Thomas Tyndale Esq. who departed this Life 13. Feb. 1671 aged 84 years and seaven months."

Monuments remaining. Chancel,

On a hatchment against S. wall. Arms of Gastrell. *Checky, argent and sable, on a chief or 3 bucksheads couped of the last. On an escutcheon of pretence,* Snell *quartering* Keynell. Crest. *A demi-lion gules gorged with a chaplet vert.*

"Memento Mori. Under those two stones lye the bodies of Nicholas Gast-rell gent., who departed this life the 15th and was buried the 20th day of February A.D. 1662, aged 83 years and 7 moneths." "Also the body of Mary, his wife who departed this life the 22ᵈ and was buried the 23ʳᵈ day of October A.D. 1661, aged 73 years and 5 months."

Against the E. wall a white marble tablet.

"Benjamin Griffin, M.A. of New Coll. Oxford, Vicar of Kington St. Michæl: Died 26 Nov. 1716, in his 39th year. His widow was 5th daughter of Sir Wm. Leche." "Also Mrs. Rose Bave, widow of Mr. Francis Bave Alder-man of Bath. She died 24 July 1734 aged 62." "Also Mrs. Hester White-lock widow, 4th dau. of Sir Wm. Leche. Died 21 Sept. 1735, aged 71."

Arms. *Sable, a chevron between 3 dolphins argent.* Griffin. Impaling *Ermine, on a chief indented gules 3 crowns or.* Leche. Crest ; *A hand grasping a snake.*

North wall. A Hatchment. *Sable, on a bend gules 3 buckles or, between 3 pheons argent.* Stubbs. Impaling, *Sable, a cross saltire, argent,* Duckett. Crest ; *an arm in armour holding a lance.* Under. the Chancel Arch, on a gravestone, Thomas Stubbs Esq.[1] of Kington.

---

1 His name as donor is on the pillars of the Church yard gates.

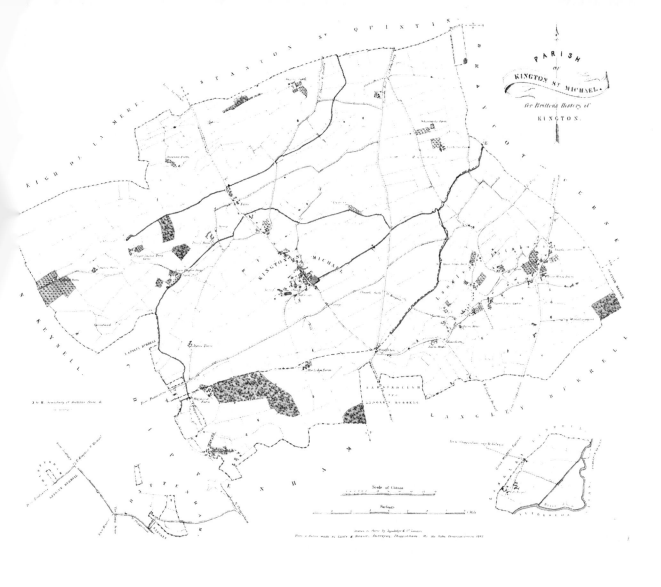

PARISH
of
KINGTON ST MICHAEL.
for Britton's History of
KINGTON.

Scale of Chains

Furlongs

Drawn in Stone by Dyneleys & C.º London.
From a Survey made by Little & Weaver, Surveyors, Chippenham, &c. the Tithe Commissioners in 1847.

St. Michael, March 1705-6 aged 53. (His wife was daughter of Wm. Duckett Esq. of Hartham, and was buried at Corsham 20 January 1712 aged 55).

NAVE. Gravestones *destroyed.*

ISAAC TAYLER of the Priory, brother to John Tayler, Vicar.

Near the Font, THOMAS LYTE of Easton Piers, great grandfather (maternally) of John Aubrey. Buried 13 May 1627, aged 96.

By him under a black marble his son ISAAC LYTE, 1659, (Aubrey's grandfather.) This inscription is still visible, but is partly concealed by a pew.

Mrs. ISRAEL LYTE his wife 1661, (Aubrey's grandmother;) daughter of Thomas Browne of Winterbourne Basset.

Gravestones *remaining.*

On a black stone very much worn, the Arms of Clifford. *Checky, a fess.*

" . . . . *Margaret* . . . . . *mes B* . . . . *Died* 19 . . . 1766, *aged* 53."

(Probably Margaret daughter of Wm. Clifford and Margaret Power, and wife of James Barrett.)

" JONATHAN DEEKE of Langley, Clothier, and Grace his wife, who having lived together in matrimony above 57 years departed this life 1699, He July 23, aged 86. She Aug. 16, aged 83.

I went before as t'was my place to do;
And I in mine soon followed you.
Nor life nor death can separate us two,
We'll hand in hand to Heaven go."

" Mrs. REBECCA KNOTT June 1760, aged 68." (sister and coheiress of Jonathan Power.) " JAMES KNOTT, gent. 1766, æt 36." JAMES POWER Junr. Gent, 1715, aged 34." " JAMES son of Nathaniel POWER and Rebecca GASTRELL: Nephew and sole heir to James son of Nicholas Gastrell and Mary his wife youngest sister and coheir to Sir Charles Snell Kt. Lord of this Manor. Died 1705, aged 44." ELIZABETH wife of James POWER senr and daughter of Jonathan Deeke of Langley in this Parish, Clothier: died October — aged 67." " JONATHAN POWER Gent. 1748. The stone placed by his sister Mrs. Sarah Coleman."

Against second column (N. side).

" WM. COLEMAN Esq. of Langley in this Parish, 1738 aged 63. SARAH his wife 1767, aged 74."

NORTH AISLE. On Tablets against the walls.

" DOROTHEA ANNE dau. of Walter COLEMAN of Langley Fitzhurst Esq. and Thermuthis his wife, 1825, aged 4 years." " THERMUTHIS wife of Walter

COLEMAN, and dau. of Robert Ashe of Langley Burrell Esq., 1825, aged 47. WALTER COLEMAN Esq., 1845, aged 67."

"ISAAC GALE of Bulidge, 1792, aged 66: and ELIZABETH his wife, daughter of Richard Michell of Langport, 1806, aged 70."

Arms. *Quarterly, 1 and 4, Azure, a fess argent fretty sable.* GALE. *2 and 3, Sable a lion rampant. — On an escutcheon of pretence, Gules a chevron or between three swans.* MICHELL.

"ISAAC SADLER GALE 1841, aged 68. Also Catharine his widow, died at Harrow 1855."

"JAMES GASTRELL gent., son and heir of Nicholas Gastrell and Mary (Snell), 1678, aged 54."

On a shield: *Or, a boar passant sable.* Crest; *a pine branch with fruit.*

"JAMES GILPIN, born in this parish in 1709. and descended from the Snells sometime Lords of the Manor. He was educated at Westminster School and elected thence to Christ Church Oxford in 1728. He afterwards settled at The Temple, and was appointed Registrar to the Dean and Chapter of Christ Church, Oxford, Auditor of their accounts, and Recorder of the same City. He died the 14th December 1766, and was buried in this churchyard."[1]

"ROBERT GLENN gent. 1775, æt. 74. Elizabeth his wife 1796, æt. 84."

"SYDENHAM TUCKER 1771, aged 58." Upon this monument

Arms. *Vert, a chevron gules charged with a mullet, between 3 rams argent.* The same on a gravestone on the floor.

"FRANCIS WHITE of Langley, 1707, æt. 73. HANNAH his 1st wife, had 11 children, 3 died young: 8 survived, viz.: Francis, John, Elizabeth, Grace, Ayliffe, Thomas, James and Lydia. AYLIFFE WHITE 1761, aged 90. ELIZABETH his wife 1758, aged 59. FRANCIS their son 1761, aged 34." ·

"SARAH wife of John PROVIS of Chippenham, dau. of James and Sarah Mascall: Sept. 1813 in 35th year."

SOUTH AISLE.

(*Destroyed.*) "JOHN POWER of Gloucester Hall, Oxford, a Practitioner in physic, 1647." (Buried, says Aubrey in his MSS., face downwards.) "NICHOLAS his brother."

(*Remaining.*) "MARY, wife of Wm. ALEXANDER of Great Somerford 1735, æt. 56." "ANNE, wife of May PINCHIN Gent. of Langley Burrell, Feb. 1721. She was one of the daughters of Richard Estcourt Gent. of Swinley in this Parish." (the rest hidden by a pew.) Arms of Estcourt.

"GEORGE EASTCOURT of Swinley, 1712. aged 29 (?)"

"DANIEL YEALFE Schoolmaster of Kington 48 years, vestry clerk 50 years, Parish clerk 16 years, 1779, aged 70. Mary his wife 1778 aged 85."

"JOHN son of Harry and Jane HITCHCOCK of All Cannings, 1820, aged 32. J. C. HITCHCOCK of Andover his son, 1841, aged 28."

---

[1] A portrait of Mr. James Gilpin is in the possession of the Misses Mascall of Allington, owners of Heywood Farm. He was a collector of Notes for the history of his native Parish, a small MS. volume of which came, through the late Mr. Britton, into the hands of the Wiltshire Archæological Society.

"RICHARD HUMPHREYS Vicar of Kington St. Michael and Rector of Draycote Cerne, 1711, aged 55. ANNE his wife, 1727, aged 68."

"JAMES MASCALL 1821, aged 80. SARAH MARTHA his wife 1821, in 79th year."

"WM. TANNER of Langley Fitzurse, 1849, aged 63."

PORCH.   Against the Wall.

"JOSEPH HINE youngest son of Richard Hine, Clerk" (and Vicar.) (rest illegible.)

CHURCH YARD.   In Aubrey's time there were tombs to

"RICHARD HINE, Clerk, and ANNE his wife. He was Vicar 50 years and upwards and died 1663 aged 78. She 1666 aged 73." ADAM MILSHAM (who gave the clock and chimes) under a tomb "the second from the South Porch towards the East." Buried 9 March 1642 aged fourscore yeares and upwards. *Citò præterit ætas.*"

Also on the South side,

"1664.

Under this tombe here doth reside, as you may well remember,
The bodie of SIMON NECK who died the 4th of November.
His age was 78 yeares, then his wife was 59,
Who dyed the last of May 47 and here she doth lye by'n."

"Honest old JOHN WASTFIELD a freeholder at Langley, 1644, above 80 years." (Aubrey.)

On the south west side of the Church yard is a raised tomb with the following inscription, now nearly effaced.

"Here lieth the body of WILLIAM HARINGTON Vicar of this Parish 34 years: who departed this life July 13, 1751, in the 64th year of his age." (with some verses, "The trumpet shall sound," &c.)   "Also SARAH his widow, died July 28, 1753, aged 59." He was son of John Harington of Kelston, Co. Somerset, by his fourth wife Helena, dau. of Benjamin Gostlett of Marshfield, Co. Glouc.: and was baptized at Kelston. His wife Sarah was dau. and coheiress of Thos. Harrison of Bath, and had no issue.

"Mrs. MARY WEBBE, 29 May 1773, aged 80."

Eastward of the Porch is a tomb to JOHN YEALFE; on a shield, *a chevron between 3 caps (?) each surmounted by a cross patteé.*

South side.

"The Rev. EDWARD ROWLANDSON, 18 years Curate of this Parish. Died 11 June 1854, aged 51." [Son of Michael John Rowlandson D.D., Vicar of Warminster. He was a Michel Fellow of Queen's Coll. Oxford, and in the second class *Lit. Hum.* 1823.]

KINGTON CROSS

Anciently stood at the turn leading down to the Priory. Aubrey says that "here in those days was a little market Fridays for fish, eggs, butter, and such small gear. Perhaps chiefly for the Nuns. The Michaelmas Fair was famous for ale and stubble geese."

I

CHARITIES.[1]

I. WOODRUFFE'S: A.D. 1664. Wm. Woodruffe of the Parish of Chippenham, yeoman, by Will dated 1 Sep. 1664, gives unto the Minister and Church-wardens of the Parish of Kington St. Michael's for the time being, a yearly Rent charge of 30 shillings: whereof ten to the Minister of Kington for preaching a Sermon on the 18th Sept. (o.s.) *in remembrance of God's mercy in preserving him in a wonderful manner from Drowning at Peckingell Bridge on the 18th Sept.* 1656. The Minister to excite the people to be mindful of mercies received, and to be thankful for the same. The other 20s. to be distributed yearly on the 18th Sept. amongst the poor people of the said Parish of Kington where there shall be most need.

The premises chargeable were a messuage, and pasture called "The Great Heth" two acres, which W. W. purchased of Samuel Unkles; and a "six acres Close" purchased of Edward Crook. All in Tytherton Lucas. A close of pasture in Chippenham called "the Breach" purchased of Wm. Bailiffe of Monkton Esq., six acres: Sheldon's Leaze eight acres: and Pipsmore twenty-five acres, lying in the Parishes of Chippenham, Langley Burrell, and Hardenhuish, purchased of Sam. Gage Chandler and Benj. Flower, Clerk: all which premises the said W. W. by Indenture of Feoffment dated 6 Nov. 1656, conveyed unto John Ely of Chippenham, Gent, and Peter Gale of Avon, yeoman, and their heirs, to the use of the said W. W. for life sans waste: and after his decease to such uses as W. W. by will in writing under his hand and seal should appoint. W. Woodruffe died 20 Jan. 1668. [In the Commissioner's Report the lands in Titherton Lucas are not noticed: those in Chippenham Parish are stated to be part of the Ivy House property, out of which the Rent charge is annually paid.]

2. LYTE'S ALMSHOUSE, A.D. 1675.

This stands on the west side of the village street, and bears the following inscription under a shield of the Founder's Arms. "Isaac

---

[1] See Charity Commissioners' Report No. 28, p. 329. The account of Woodruffe's Charity is taken from the MSS. of Mr. James Gilpin, a Barrister, and by him extracted from Parish Evidences, now apparently missing.

Lyte, born in this Parish, Alderman of London late deceased, built this Almshouse and endowed it A.D. 1675." He resided at Mortlake in Surrey, and by his Will, proved 21 Aug. 1673, bequeathed " six hundred pounds to be laid out in building an Almeshouse in the Parish of Keinton in the C⁰· of Wilts where I was born, for the maintenance of Six poor men to be from time to time nominated and appointed by the Minister, and Churchwardens, and the major part of the most sufficient men in that Parish. And my Will is, that the money be received by Richard Poole and Mr. Jonathan Dyke, and by them to be first laid out for the use aforesaid." A site for the House and piece of land for gardens, were conveyed to Trustees in 1674 and again in 1707: in which year also an interest in 50 acres in the Parish of Corston was vested in the same parties under the charitable trusts in Lyte's Will. In 1730 the whole premises were again assigned to Trustees: of whom Mr. Isaac Sadler Gale of Bath considered himself surviving representative in 1811. Partly with his own money, partly with the funds of the Charity, he put the Almshouse in proper order, and then claimed the nominations; but the claim was resisted by the Parish authorities. The land at Corston has been for many years in the possession of the Earl Radnor: the tenant paying only £20 a year to Kington Almshouse. Why this sum was fixed upon there is no satisfactory explanation : and the Commissioners in their Report mark the case as one proper for the consideration of the Attorney General, but nothing has been done. The Almshouses form one building, consisting of six tenements of two rooms each.

NEWMAN'S (or SADLER'S) c. A.D. 1680.

The founder of this Charity was Miss Dorothy Newman, eldest niece of Sir Charles Snell. She died unmarried before 1680, giving £200 to the Poor. Her representatives were her three nieces, Dorothy Sadler wife of Wm. Coleman, Meriell Sadler, (afterwards wife of Isaac Gale), and Margaret Sadler, (afterwards wife of Thos. Stokes). In 1680 each of the three settled a rent charge on certain lands to maintain the charity. Two of these are now payable by Mr. Walter Coleman of Langley, and the third by the representatives of Mr. Isaac Sadler Gale. Six pounds a year distributed in bread on St. Thomas's day.

4. TAYLOR'S, A.D. 1729.

A Rent charge of 20s. a year under the Will of Mr. Thomas Taylor dated 18th Sept. 1727, now payable out of land in Langley belonging to Viscount Wellesley. Distributed in bread amongst the poor on St. Thomas's day.

5. BOWERMAN'S, A.D. 1730.

Mrs. Sarah Bowerman by Will dated 6th Dec. 1730, gave £5 a year for ever, payable by the Trustees of Christ's Hospital, London, to the Schoolmaster at Kington St. Michael towards the education of poor children.

6. WHITE'S GIFT, A.D. 1821.

Mr. Thomas White of London, by Will dated 21st January 1821, gave to the Minister and Churchwardens for the time being £200 for the better maintenance of the poor inhabitants of the Almshouses. The Dividends on £259 7s. 4d. Three per cent Reduced Annuities are accordingly so applied.

AUBREY AND BRITTON.

In the annals of a country parish it is a rare thing to find even a solitary name that has earned for itself more than local and temporary celebrity. The builder of a Church, a great House, or a School, or the Founder of a Charity, may, with the help of a monument, prolong for a few years the fact of his connection with the place; but even this kind of reputation, sometimes expensively purchased, dies away by degrees. One generation enters whilst another makes its exit, and like wave after wave spreading out upon the shore, each absorbs imperceptibly the traces of the last.

But in the chronicle of Births in this parish, are written *two* names, now known far and wide beyond its limits. Born, as to time, within 146 years; as to distance, within a mile, of each other; JOHN AUBREY and JOHN BRITTON have obtained a place amongst English literati as the earliest labourers in the neglected field of Wiltshire Topography: and the latter, for works of a more general

kind. In the present memoir they are accordingly entitled to especial notice.

John Aubrey F.R.S.

Without committing the error either of over-rating or under-rating Aubrey, whatever else he might be, he was certainly an original.[1] Though his writings ·present a strange farrago, they have nevertheless preserved many curious facts that otherwise would have been lost. His notes and memoranda of persons and places jotted down at the time and on the spot, whether on horseback, or in a village church, or at the tables of his friends, have now become, through lapse of years, useful to antiquaries and genealogists: affording a clue to accurate information if not conveying it themselves. To method and finish he makes no sort of pretension, but simply tells what he saw or what he heard, whenever and wherever it fell in his way. His anecdotes if not always historically correct in every particular, are probably as near.the truth as most anecdotes. At all events they are told without any malicious colouring, with much good humour and quaint simplicity. To be critically severe upon Aubrey, considering his character and occupations, and the various domestic distractions under which he followed them, is simply ridiculous. Yet he has been very harshly dealt with; by no one more than Antony Wood, who, after 25 years acquaintance, could find it in his heart thus to describe his deceased, but to the last, forgiving friend. "He was a shiftless person, roving and magotie-headed, and sometimes little better than crazed: and being exceedingly credulous would stuff his many letters sent to A. W. with folliries and misinformations which would sometimes guide him into the paths of error."[2] The circumstance which is believed to have provoked so splenetic an effusion, was this. In the second volume of his "Athenæ Oxonienses," Wood had been bold enough to put forth an undisguised intimation that the late Chancellor (Lord Clarendon) had not scrupled to receive bribes for preferment. For this *scandalum magnatum*

---

[1] See some account of him in Vol. I. p. 32.
[2] Ath. Oxon. Bliss's Edit. Life, p. lx.

proceedings were taken against him. He was fined and degraded, and the volume containing the alleged libel was publicly burnt. Smarting under this disgrace Wood poured the vial of his wrath upon Aubrey, from one of whose private letters he had adopted this charge against the Chancellor. But he ought rather to have been angry with himself for having been so imprudent as to adopt and print what it was quite in his power to have suppressed. The offensive passage that led to so much trouble occurred in Wood's "Life of Judge Jenkins," in which he said: "After the restoration of King Charles II. t'was expected by all that he (Jenkins) would be made one of the Judges in Westminster Hall, and so he might have been, would he have given money to the then Lord Chancellor." The original letter from Aubrey to Wood from which the latter borrowed this statement—almost word for word, is preserved in the Ashmolean Library. It is dated London, January 16, 1671. After other memoranda for the "Life of Judge Jenkins," Aubrey continues thus: "T'was pitty he was not made one of the Judges of Westminster Hall, and he might have been, *(he told me,)* if he would have given money to the Chancellor: but he scorned it . . . Mr. T. H. Malms^br. " (Thos. Hobbes of Malmesbury) "told him (Jenkins) one day at dinner, that that hereafter would not show well for somebodie's Honour in History." The story therefore against Clarendon, whether true or false, was Judge Jenkins's own: and if Wood chose to print it, he had no one but himself to blame for the consequences.

One or two other critics have echoed A. Wood's abuse, and amongst them, Dr. Farmer in his Essay upon the learning of Shakspeare. Aubrey had preserved a few anecdotes (and it is to be wished he had collected more) of the early life of the great Dramatist. These Dr. Farmer scouts, but rather unjustly; for Aubrey only repeated what "he had been told by some of the neighbours at Stratford." He was a truthful man and no inventor: generally gave his authority for his stories, and though perhaps they may be sometimes such as we are unwilling to believe, still they were the current stories of the day. Aubrey was born only nine years after Shakspeare died: near enough, one would suppose, to have enabled him to gather a multitude of facts that now would have been invaluable. That he has not done so, considering his propensity that way, perhaps was owing to lack of such materials: which if it were the case, only increases the mystery that surrounds the name of Shakspeare.

Aubrey may have been credulous and not free from superstitions shared by men of finer intellect than himself: but it is owing to this very credulity that he has left us many things characteristic of the times. He was, it is said, regarded as a good Naturalist. He certainly noticed the iron ore at Seend near Devizes, only now, after 200 years, beginning to be worked.[1] He made many other clever remarks on Geology, long before the principles of that Science were systematically laid down: pointed out mineral springs that became afterwards, and for a while, popular: and though much of his "Natural History" may read very oddly at the present time, it seems to have been fully up to the mark of the Science of his own. The same may be said of his Antiquarian gatherings. He used his eyes and pen when others were blind and idle. The ruins of Avebury are not known to have been mentioned by any English writer till his attention had been accidentally called to them. In

---

[1] "Seend *(vulgo Seene)* is a very well built village on a sandy hill, from whence it has its name; *sand* being in the old English called *send* (for so I find writt in the records of the Tower): as also Send, in Surrey, is called for the same reason. Underneath this sand (not very deep, in some place of the highway not above a yard or a yard and a half), *I discovered the richest iron ore that ever I saw or heard of.* Come there on a certain occasion (at the Revell A.D. 1666), it rained at 12 or one of the clock very impetuously, so that it had washed away the sand from the ore; and walking out to see the country, about 3 p.m., the sun shining bright reflected itself from the ore to my eyes. Being surprised at so many spangles, I took up the stone with a great deal of admiration. I went to the smith, Geo. Newton, an ingenious man, who from a blacksmith turned clock-maker and fiddle-maker, and he assured me that he has melted of this ore in his forge, which the ore of the Forest of Dean, &c., will not do.

"The reader is to be advertized that the forest of Melksham did extend itself to the foot of this hill. It was full of goodly oaks, and so near together that they say a squirrell might have leaped from tree to tree. It was disafforested about 1635, and the oaks were sold for 1s. or 2s. per boord at the most; and then *nobody ever took notice of this iron ore,* which, as I said before, every sun-shine day after a rousing shower, glistered in their eyes. Now there is scarce an oak left in the whole parish, and oaks are very rare all hereabout, so that this rich mine cannot be melted and turned to profit." (Nat. Hist. of Wilts, p. 21.)

January 1649, his 24th year, being out hunting with Lord Francis Seymour near Marlborough, the hounds ran through the village of Avebury: "In the closes there (he says) I was wonderfully surprised at the sight of those *vast stones of which I had never heard before,*" (though within 15 miles of his home) "as also of the mighty bank and graffe about it." He left the company, and having examined the place, rejoined them at Kennet. Upon subsequent visits he made his notes. And until that time, this extraordinary monument, which if, whilst yet entire, it had been made national property and protected from injury, would have been now the most extraordinary one in the world, does not appear to have been even named in any English book extant.

Aubrey's "Lives of Eminent Men," originally written in aid of Antony Wood's labours, were published (with some suppressions) for the first time at Oxford in 1813, by Dr. Bliss and the Rev. J. Walker; in a work called "Letters from the Bodleian." They refer for the most part either to contemporaries and personal acquaintances of his own (and he seems to have known every body,) or to persons of a certain public station who, immediately before his time, had pronounced their "Valete et plaudite" upon the stage of life. In these "Lives" there is nothing elaborate or artificial. They are merely memoranda of character and manners, without concealment of the bad or exaggeration of the good: anecdotes, odd sayings and doings, all naturally told, and such as more digni-fied biographers would hardly have introduced. But it is this very *naïveté* which makes them the more amusing. Aubrey's "eminent men" are not drawn in full ceremonial costume to produce an im-posing effect, but in their every day dress, and sometimes in their undress. In his description something is sure to be found, not to be found any where else: and much as he has been reviled by stiff critics who would fain make the world believe, that wise men and heroes were heroes and wise men at all hours of their lives, his anecdotes are in the main perfectly credible. Slips of memory in names of person or place may be frequent: and there is inaccuracy in trifling facts: but as no two persons ever tell the same story in precisely the same words, Aubrey's aberrations in narrative are not peculiar. A writer of the present day, Mr. Charles Knight, has taken a more generous view of the "Lives"; a work which, it should always be remembered, was never revised or prepared for the press by Aubrey himself. "There are few books that I take up more willingly in a vacant half hour than the scraps of biography which Aubrey, the Wiltshire Antiquarian, addressed to Antony à Wood. These little fragments are so quaint and characteristic of the writer: so sensible in some passages and so absurd in others: so full of what may be called the Prose of Biography, with reference to the objects of historical and literary reverence, and so encomiastic with regard to others whose memories have wholly perished in the popular view, that I shall endeavour to look at them consecutively as singular examples of what a clever man thought of his contemporaries, and of others famous in his day, whether their opinions accord with, or are opposed to our present estimate."[1]

Aubrey having been at first and for a long time known as a writer, only by his "Miscellanies," a collection formed in days when Astrology was popular, and therefore containing much that is fantastic and irrational, no wonder that he obtained in later times the reputation of a dreamy visionary. But though he tells us in that book what foolish things other people believed and reported, it does not follow that he really believed them all: any more than that any writer who should now transmit to future times the spirit-rappings and table-turnings of the present day, would be obliged to have faith in those tricks himself. His turn of mind being no doubt superstitious, and his fancy leading him to such studies, he appeared to be more so than probably was the case. But letting all infirmities pass, his true merit is this. In days when there were neither books, nor students, nor societies, nor taste for English antiquities, he was a pioneer single-handed in that department: and for what he did, according to the best of his ability, his name deserves to be held in kind remembrance, especially in the County of Wilts.

A list of his various writings, some published and others still in manuscript, is given in Mr. Britton's Memoir of him, published by the Wiltshire Topographical Society in 1845, p. 83. The

---

[1] "Once upon a Time," vol. I. p. 296.

Monumenta Britannica" mentioned there (p.89) as missing, has since
been discovered in the Bodleian Library. A fourth edition of his
"Miscellanies" has appeared during the present year[1] with the
addition of the Preface designed by Aubrey for his History of
Wilts, and printed in "Curll's Miscellanies" 1714.

He was a thoroughly unsettled and unlucky man. His whole
inheritance (at one time £700 a year) was consumed in paying
debts and defending actions transmitted with his estate. He lived
chiefly at Broad Chalk, sometimes at Easton; kept terms in London,
and spent much time riding over Wiltshire in search, now of
"Antiq.", now of a wife. The one he found; the other, not.
Through sundry mishaps, his

> "—— course of true love never did run smooth.
> For either it was difference in blood,
> Or else misgraffed in respect of years,
> Or else it stood upon the choice of friends,
> Or, if there were a sympathy in choice,
> *Law*, death or sickness did lay siege to it."

In this reference to Lysander's catalogue of obstacles,[2] the change
of reading (acknowledged in Italic type,) is specially required for
Aubrey's case; his principal suit to the fair sex in the person of Mistress Joan Sumner of Seend, having been suddenly extinguished by a
suit at law, the full particulars and cause whereof are lost to curiosity. His assiduities also to others invariably ended in disappoint-
ment. Just at the interesting moment the "natal star" was always
found to be in provoking opposition, and so it came to pass that he
never lived to pay for license or be *called* in church.

His birth-place and family connexion (on his mother's side) with
Kington St. Michael's have been mentioned above (p. 79). The
"Accidents" of his life will be most properly given in his own
words, copied from loose and vague notes amongst his MSS., forming all that is left of his

AUTOBIOGRAPHY.
I.A.

"To be interponed as a sheet of wast paper only at the binding

[1] 12mo. Russell Smith, Soho Square, 1857.
[2] Midsummer Night's Dream, Act. 1.

of a booke. This person's life is more remarqueable in an Astrologicall respect for his escape from many dangers in journeys both by land and water, than for any advancement of learning, having, from his birth (till of late yeares) being labouring under a crowd of ill directions. He was borne at Easton Pierse (a hamlet in the parish of Kington St. Michael), in the Hundred of Malmsbury, in the Countie of Wilts, (his Mother's inheritance, D. and H. of Mr. Isaac Lyte,) about sun-rising on March 12 (St. Gregory's day), A.D. 1625.[1] In an ill hour, Saturn directly opposing my ascendant—in

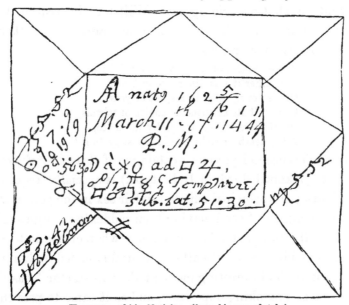

Horoscope of his Nativity, (from his own sketch.)

my Grandfather's chamber I first drew my breath: very weak and like to dye, and therefore christened that morning before morning prayer.

---

[1] A mistake has sometimes been made (amongst others, by the Editor of "Notes and Queries, vol. I. p. 13) about Aubrey's birthday; arising from a passage in his "Miscellanies" ("Day-Fatality"): "I shall take particular notice here of the *3rd of November, because it is my own Birthday, &c.*" But the early pages of the "Miscellanies" including this passage are stated by Aubrey himself to have been copied word for word from "Observations by John Gibbon" (Blue-Mantle), printed 1678; (and also Harl. Misc. viii. 300, 8vo). The 3rd November was therefore *John Gibbon's* birthday, not Aubrey's. He was certainly baptized at Kington (see *Parish Register*) on 12th March: and in allusion to this day he frequently subscribed his name in letters to his friends as "J. Gregorius."

"1629. About 3 years old I had a grievous ague, I can remember it. I got not health till eleven or twelve. This sickness nipt my strength in the bud. Longævous healthy kindred. When a boy—bred ignorant at Eston [eremiticall solitude]: was very curious: his greatest delight was, to be with the artificers that came there, joyners, carpenters, cowpers, masons, and understand their trades. *Horis vacuis*, (at leisure hours) I drew and painted. Did ever love to converse with old men as Living Histories; cared not for play.

"Anno 1633. I entered into my Grammar at the Latin School at Yatton Kaynell, in the Church, where the Curate, Mr. Hart, taught the eldest boys, Virgil, Ovid, &c. The fashion then was to save the forules of their bookes with a false cover of parchment, sc. old manuscript, which I was too young to understand; but I was pleased with the elegancy of the writing and the coloured initials. I remember the Rector (Mr. Wm. Stump, great gr. son of Stump the Cloathier of Malmsbury,) had severall manuscripts of the Abbey. He was a proper man, and a good fellow, and when he brewed a barrell of special ale, his use was to stop the bunghole (under the clay) with a sheet of manuscript. He said nothing did it so well, which it grieved me then to see. I remember having learnt the Alphabet from a Horn book, now extinct.

"1634. Afterwards I went to School to Mr. Robert Latimer, a delicate and little person, Rector of Leigh Delamere—a mile—fine walk —who had an easie way of teaching: and every time we asked leave to go forth we had a Latin word from him, which at our return we were to tell him again. This in a little while amounted to a good number of words. Zeal to learning extraordinary: but memory not tenacious. Mr. Latimer, at 70, wore a dudgeon,[1] with a knife and bodkin, as also my old grandfather Lyte and Alderman Whitson of Bristowe, which I suppose was the common fashion in their young dayes.

" Here was like covering of bookes. In my grandfather's days

---

[1] A small dagger. " It was a serviceable dudgeon, either for fighting or for drudging:" Hudibras. Properly the root of box of which handles were made. (Halliwell). The handle, in Macbeth; "on thy blade and dudgeon."

the manuscripts flew about like butterflies. All musick books, account books, copy books, &c., were covered with old manuscripts, as wee cover them now with blew or marble paper; and the glovers at Malmsbury made great havock of them : and gloves were wrapt up no doubt in many good pieces of antiquity. Before the late warres a world of rare manuscripts perished hereabouts : for within half a dozen miles of this place were the Abbies of Malmsbury, Bradenstoke, Stanleigh, Farleigh, Bath, and Cirencester.

"This summer 1634, (I remember it was venison season, July or Aug.) Mr. Thos. Hobbes[1] came into his native country to visit his friends, and amongst others he came to see his old Schoolmaster, Mr. Latimer at Leigh Delamere, when I was then a little youth at school in the church, newly entered into my grammar by him. Here was the first place and time that I ever had the honour to see this worthy learned man, who was then pleased to take notice of me, and the next day came and visited my relations. He was a proper man, briske, and in very good equipage: his haire was then quite black. He stayed at Malmsbury and in the neighbourhood a weeke or better; twas the last time that ever he was in Wiltshire.[2]

"When a boy, never riotous or prodigal:—of inventive and philosophical head : my witt was always working, but not to verse. —Exceeding mild of spirit, mighty susceptible of fascination.

---

[1] The " Philosopher ; " a native of Malmsbury, author of Leviathan, &c.

[2] Some biographers have said that Hobbes and Aubrey were school-*fellows*. This is clearly wrong, as Hobbes was born in 1588, 37 years before Aubrey : but they had the same Master, though at different times and places. Mr. Latimer in early life kept a private school in Westport, Malmsbury, when Hobbes was his pupil. In 1609 he became Rector of Leigh Delamere. Against the base of the East Wall of the Church outside, on a stone (removed from the inside when it was rebuilt in 1846) is the following inscription. "Here lyeth Robert Latymer, sometime Rector and Pastor of this Church : who deceased this life the 2d day of November A.D. 1634." The Rectory house was taken down and rebuilt on the same site in 1639 : and underwent the same process again in 1846: but under the floor of the study in which this memoir of Kington St. Michael's and Aubrey is now written by one of Mr. Latimer's successors, are buried the two floors of the former houses ; the lowest (of plaster) would probably be that on which Aubrey as a boy repeated his Latin words, or got his slice of the venison with which the Philosopher's visit to Leigh Delamere appears to have been celebrated.

"T'was my unhappiness in half a year to lose this good enformer (Mr. Latimer) by his death: and afterwards was under severall dull ignorant teachers till 12; 1638: about which time I was sent to Blandforde School in Dorset; W. Sutton B.D.: who was ill-natured. Here I recovered my health and got Latin and Greeke.

"1638. Here also was the use of covering of bookes with old parchments, sc. leases, &c., but I never saw any thing of a Manuscript there. Hereabout were no Abbeys or convents for men. Anno 1647, I went to Parson Stump out of curiosity, to see his Manuscripts, whereof I had seen some in my childhood: but by that time they were all lost and disperst. His sons were gunners and souldiers, and scoured their gunnes with them: but he showed me severall old deedes granted by the Lords Abbotts with their seals annexed, which I suppose his sonne, Capt. John Stump of Malmsbury hath still.

"I was always enquiring of my (maternal) Grandfather (Isaac Lyte), of the old time, the Roodloft, ceremonies of the Priory, &c. At 8 I was a kind of engineer and fell then to Drawing, beginning with plain outlines in draughts of the curtains: then on to colours; being only my own instructor. Copied pictures in the parlour, in a table-book. At 9, a portraiter and was passable. Was wont to lament with myself that I lived not in a city, where I might have access to watchmakers, locksmiths, &c. Not much care for grammar. Strong and early impulse to Antiquities. Tacitus and Juvenal. Look't through some logique and ethiques. A musical inventive head: ideas were clear.

"1639. My uncle's nag ran away with me, Monday after Easter, and gave me a very dangerous fall. About this time my grandfather Aubrey dyed, leaving my Father, who was not educated to learning but to hawking.

"1642, May 3. Entered at Trinity Coll. Oxon. Peace. 'Atque inter sylvas Academi quærere verum.' But now did Bellona thunder: and as a clear sky is sometimes overstretched with a dismall black cloud, so was the serene peace by the Civill War through the factions of those times. 'Amovêre loco me tempora grato.' In August following, 1643, my Father sent for me home for feare.

'Religio Medici' first opened my understanding, I carried it to Easton, with Sir Kenelm Digby. In Feb. following (with much importunity) I gott my Father to lett me go to beloved Oxford againe, (then a garrison pro Rege). I got Mr. Hesketh a priest, Mr. Dobson's man, to draw the Ruines of Oseney 2 or 3 wayes before t'was pulled downe: now the very foundation is digged up.

"April and May. The small pox at Oxford. Left that ingeniose place, and for 3 years led a sad life in the country.—where I conversed with none but servants and rustiques, (to my great greefe, for in those days fathers were not acquainted with their children) and soldiers quartered. Odi profanum vulgus et arceo. It was a most sad life to me then, in the prime of my youth, nott to have the benefit of an ingeniouse conversation, and scarce any good bookes. Almost a consumption. This sad life I did lead in the country till 1646, at which time I got (with much adoe) leave of my father to let me goe to the Middle Temple.

"1646, April 16. Admitted. But my Father's sickness and business never permitted me to make any settlement to my study. My fancy lay most to geometry. My studies in it were on horseback, &c., so I got my Algebra: Oughtred in my pocket, with a little information from Edw. Davenant D.D. of Gillingham, Dorset. [See Lives II. 296.] My father discouraged me. My head was never idle: alwaies working: and even travelling (from 1649 to 1670 was never off my horseback) did gleane some observations, of which I have a collection in folio of two quire of paper, some whereof are to be valued. If ever I had been good for anything 'twould have been a Painter. I could fancy a thing so strongly, and have so cleare an idea of it.

"June 24 following, Oxon was surrendered, and there came to London many of the King's party, with whom I grew acquainted (many of them I knew before). I loved not debauches, but their martiall conversation: was not so fit for the messe.

"November 6. I returned to Trin. Coll. in Oxon, again, to my great joy: was much made of by the Fellows, had their learned conversation, look't on books, musique. Here and at Middle Temple off and on I for the most part enjoyed the greatest felicity of my life, (Ingeniose youths like rosebudds imbibe the morning dew.) till

"1648, Dec. Xmas eve, I was sent for home again to my sick father, who never recovered: where I was engaged to look after his country business and solicit a law suit.

1649-50, April. My Mother fell from her horse and brake her arm the last day of April, when I was a suitor to Mistress Jane Codrington.

"1651. About the 16 or 18 April I sawe that incomparable good conditioned gentlewoman, Mistress M. Wiseman, with whom at first sight I was in love.

"Oct. 21. · My Father died, leaving me debts £1800: and law proceedings £1000. Began to enter into pocket mem. books philosophicall and antiquarian remarques A.D. 1654 at Llantrihid.

"Sept, 1655, or rather I think 1656, I began my chargeable and tedious lawe suite on the entaile at Brecknockshire and Monmouthshire. This yeare and the last was a strange yeare to me. Several love and law suites.

"1657. Nov. 27. Obiit Domina Kasker Ryves, with whom I was to marry: to my great losse.—£2000; besides counting one of her Brothers £1000 per ann.

"A°. . . I made my Will, and settled my estate on Trustees, intending to have seen the Antiq. of Rome and Italy, and then to have returned and married. But (Diis aliter visum est superis) viz. . . . to my inexpressible grief and ruine hindered the designe . . . But notwithstanding all these embarrassments, I did, *pian piano* (as they occurred) take notes of Antiq., and having a quick draught have drawn landskips on horseback symbolically, as on the journey to Ireland A.D. 1660.

1659. March or April: like to break my neck in Ely Minster: and the next day riding a gallop there, my horse tumbled over and over, and yet I, thank God, no hurt."

[After visiting Ireland and being nearly shipwrecked at Holyhead, he sold his Burleton estate in Herefordshire to Dr. F. Willis: then the Manor of Stratford,[1] in 1661 and 1662. In 1663 he was elected F.R.S. In June 1664, he went to France, was very ill at

---

[1] Probably Stretford near Leominster.

Orleans, and returned in October. Another bad fall from his horse, Monday after Christmas.]

"1665. Nov. 1. I made my first address (in an ill hour) to Joan Sumner. She lived with her Brother at Seend. The next year was still more unlucky. 1666. This year all my business and affairs ran kim kam: nothing tooke effect, as if I had been under an ill tongue, treacheries and enmities in abundance against me. 1667. December. Arrested in Chancery-lane at Mistress Sumner's suit."

In February following he obtained with some difficulty a verdict against her, with £600 damages, in a trial at Salisbury; but the amount was reduced to £300 on a new trial at Winchester. In 1669, March 5, this trial came on; lasting from 8 to 9. One Peter Gale maliciously contrived to arrest him just before, but the trick failed. He attributed the result of the trial to the "Judge being exceeding made against him by my Lady Hungerford, (of Corsham)."[1]

In 1669-70, after being owner 17 years, he sold his Easton Piers Farm; and his interest in the farm at Broad Chalk. The latter had belonged to the Abbey of Wilton: and was held by the Aubreys as lessees under the Earls of Pembroke. To Antony à Wood on the 2nd October 1669, he writes "I shall be the next weeke at Easton Piers, where I should be glad to heare from you by the Bristowe Carrier in Jesus College Lane, to be left at Michaell's Kington." It was during this visit that he made the Drawings of his Villa referred to above, (p. 79). On the 28th April following he was again there, and perhaps for the last time of residence, the Farm being transferred to the new owner, Mr. Sherwin,[2] at Lady Day 1671. Aubrey

[1] In his letters to A. Wood, Aubrey names another person as a chief in the conspiracy to defeat his advances to Mistress Sumner. "Dec. 1668. The person that you mentioned in your letter that is now Lancaster Herald, his name is Chaloner, whose character I have heard of by one of his neighbours that liveth at the Devizes. He hath been an officer in the army, a bustling man for the world: of great acquaintance with the Gentry and one that understandeth his trade well. He will not stick to ask enough" (for the resignation of his place). "He is one that the Office" (of Heralds) "and I think every body hates, or ought to do, if they knew him as well as I doe: for he hath been the *boutefeu* (firebrand) to sett my dame and me at variance."

[2] Also purchaser of the Priory. He left both during Aubrey's life time to a daughter and heir. N. H. of W. p. 119.

looked upon this as an ominous event; noted the day and hour, and drew a horoscope. "25 March 1671. One P.M. Possession given by Jonathan Rogers to Mr. Sherwin;" and in his Nat. Hist. of Wilts, p. 119, ("Fatalities and Places") thus alludes to the sale. "Several places in this county have been fortunate to their owners. Contrarywise there are some unlucky. Easton Piers hath had six owners, since the reign of Henry VII.: where I myself had a share to act my part. One part of it called Lyte's Kitchen hath been sold four times over since 1630." He appears to have realized by the sale of Easton and Broad Chalk less than he expected by "£500, plus £200 goods and timber."

Having now been obliged, from "debts, lawsuits, oppositions, refusals, and perpetual riding," to part with the whole of his property "I absconded as a banished man. Ubi? In monte Dei videbitur."[1] I was in as much affliction as a mortal could be: and never quiet till all was gone;[2] submitted myselfe to God's will: wholly cast myselfe on God's providence. I wished Monasterys had not been put down, that the Reformers would have been more moderate as to that point. Fit there should have been receptacles for contemplative men. If of 500 but one or two. What a pleasure t'would have been to have travelled from monastery to monastery. The Reformers in the Lutheran Countries were more prudent than to destroy them, as in Alsatia, &c. Nay, the Turks have monasteries: why should our Reformers be so severe? Providence raysed me (unexpectedly) good friends: the Rt. Hon.

---

[1] i.e. "Where? In the mount of the Lord it shall be seen." Alluding to the meaning of the name "Jehovah-jireh" (Gen. xxii. 14.) viz., "The Lord will provide."

[2] In his unpublished letters to Anthony Wood (preserved in the Ashmolean Museum) Aubrey "still harps" upon his favourite maternal acres.

1671. "I am much beholding to you for the honour that you are pleased to let my name live. Pray putt in my beloved Easton Pierse—where and to what estate I was born. If heaven had pleased I might have enjoyed it." In another "I humbly thank you for the honour that you intend me by inserting my name in your living and lasting History. I desire you to name me of Easton Pierse: to contradistinguish me from other John Aubreys: it being the place where I was born, and my Mother's inheritance which my cruel Fate enforced me to part with. A most lovely seate it is."

Nicholas Earl of Thanet, with whom I was delitescent" (in retirement) "at Hethfield in Kent, near a year. Edmund Wyld Esq., R.S.S., of Glazely Hall, Salop, tooke me into his arms, with whom I most commonly take my diet and sweet otiums. Makes me lethargique."

"Aᵒ 1671 : having sold all and disappointed as aforesaid of moneys I received, I had so strong an impulse to (in good part) finish the Description of Wilts, in 2 volumes in folio, that I could not be quiet 'until I had done it, and that with danger enough, 'tanquam canis e Nilo,'[1] for feare of crocodiles—i.e. catchpoles. And indeed all that I have done and that little I have studied, has been just after that fashion : so that had I not lived long my want of leisure would have afforded a slender harvest. A strange fate that I have laboured under, never in my life to enjoy one entire moneth—(once at Chalke in my absconding)—or 6 weeks otium for contemplation."

Besides Mr. Wyld and the Earl of Thanet he had other friends who gave him shelter and hospitality, viz.: at Lavington, the Earl of Abingdon, to whose first wife (by descent from Danvers) he was related: and at Draycot, Sir James Long. Of this gentleman he always writes in terms of great respect as his "ever honoured friend." A similarity in tastes and pursuits appears from their correspondence, as well as from the frequent recurrence amongst Aubrey's papers of " Quære Sir J. L."[2] He had also in the neighbourhood of Easton a great coadjutor in Thomas Gore Esq., of Alderton, a

---

[1] " Like a dog by the Nile": Running and lapping for fear of being caught.

[2] "I should now be both orator and soldier to give this honoured friend of mine, a gentleman absolute in all numbers, his due character. Only son of Sir Walter Long: born at South Wraxhall in Wilts, Westminster Scholar; of Magd. Coll. Oxon. Went to France. Married a most elegant beauty and wit, dau. of Sir E. L. 25 æt. (Dorothy d. of Sir Edw. Leach of Shipley, Co. Derby.) In the Civil Wars Col. of horse in Sir F. Dodington's brigade. Good swordsman: admirable extempore orator : great memory: great historian and romancer : great falconer and for horsemanship. For insects exceedingly curious, and searching long since in natural things. Oliver, Protector, hawking at Hounslow Heath discoursing with him fell in love with his company, and commanded him to wear his sword, and to meet him a-hawking : which made the strict cavaliers look on him with an evil eye. Scripsit " History and causes of the Civil Warre." [Lives. II. 433.]

country gentleman of independent fortune and good education, whose fancy lay towards genealogical pursuits, chiefly Heraldry: on which subject whenever Aubrey is at a loss, his intention to consult the Alderton oracle is expressed by a "Mem. to ask T. G. de hoc."

In a curious folio manuscript history of his own family by Mr. Gore (now in the possession of Mr. Poulett Scrope), it is mentioned that at some period before the year 1664 Aubrey had mortgaged his estate at Broad Chalk to Thos. Gore and his brother Charles, as Trustees to their sister Anna, afterwards wife of John Scrope Esq. of Castle Combe.[1]

Another literary friend from whose society he found much comfort in the latter part of his life, was Mr. (afterwards Bishop) Tanner, a native of Market Lavington, author of the Notitia Monastica. Tanner was only 22 years old at Aubrey's death, but he had already shown so many qualifications for undertaking an important historical and topographical work, as to lead Aubrey to express the hope that in him the County of Wilts might find a proper historian.

The following is his own list of the persons with whom (besides those already mentioned) he had been most intimate.

A. Ettrick of Trin. Coll. Oxford. Francis Potter, Rector of Kilmington near Mere, of whom, as a very ingenious mathematician and mechanic, Aubrey gives a long account in his "Lives,"

---

1 At a later period the friendship between T. Gore and Aubrey appears to have been worn threadbare: for of his former colleague, Aubrey in his fatal year 1671, writes thus, (to A. Wood). "Pray remember me to Mr. Browne," (a clerical antiquary and friend). "If he writes or sees Mr. Gore, let him not tell him that he saw me: for he is a fidling peevish fellow, and something related to my adversaries." Again, in the same year when absconding, "I writ a line to Mr. Gore a little before I went into France (that is, to Kent) to quære some things: and to know what the Heralds did, &c., and told him that I correspond with you and that you could send a letter to me. If he should not assist me he were an ill-natured cur, for he hath made me as much his slave as Sir Browne." Finally, in 1680. "Pray write to the cuckold at '*Alderton, alias Aldrington*' to enquire, &c., &c. But he is a yare man and afraid of my queries as many people are when we want to preserve the memories of their Relations." Aubrey here alludes to Mr. Gore's preciseness in expression, certainly carried to a wearisome excess; for every time he names his own parish in the MS. family History above referred to, (and the name occurs a dozen times in every page) he invariably reiterates his "Alderton alias Aldrington."

vol. ii. p. 496. Jo. Lydall of the Middle Temple. Sir John Hoskins Bart., grandson of the celebrated Winchester versifier Serjeant Hoskins.[1] Edmund Wyld Esq. of Glazely Hall. Robert Hooke of Gresham Coll. (Lives ii. 403.) Thos. Hobbes, (Do. ii. 592, a very long memoir written at Hobbes's special request). Antony Wood. Bishop Seth Ward, of Sarum. (Lives ii. 571.) Dr. Wm. Holder. (Do. ii. 397.) Sir Wm. Petty "my singular friend." (Do. ii. 481.) Mr. Charles Seymour (Lord S. of Trowbridge). Sir Lionel Jenkins.

His notes of his own life conclude thus: "I now indulge my genius with my friends, and pray for the young angel's rest, at Mrs. More's near Gresham College."[2] He survived the loss of his property 26 years: and after the usual course of declining health, died suddenly at Oxford on his way to Draycote, and was buried in the Church of St. Mary Magdalene.[3] The entry in the Register stands thus "1697. John Aubrey, a stranger, was buried June 7." Without either brass or marble there or elsewhere, to preserve his memory, the name of the good-natured Antiquary of Easton Piers has nevertheless flitted from tongue to tongue: and the well worn condition of his manuscripts in the Ashmolean Museum bears ample witness to the homage of his votaries.

Several portraits of him were made at different periods of life. The only one now known is a miniature by Faithorne, preserved at Oxford, taken in 1666 when he was 40 years old, an engraving of which accompanies this Memoir.

---

[1] The writer of this Memoir has ventured (in "Notes and Queries" vol. vi. p. 495) to claim for this "Serjeant Hoskins" the authorship of the verses on the *Trusty Servant*, so well known to all Winchester Scholars. And this, on the authority of Aubrey, who in one of his letters to A. Wood (Oct. 27, 1671,) (amongst a great number lately arranged in the Ashmolean Library) mentions the "*picture of the Servant, and the Latin Verses at Winton, done by The Serjeant when he went to school there, but now firmly painted.*" Hoskins was at Winchester School in 1584 and died 1638. He was well known for his dexterity in Latin and English Epigrams and Epitaphs, as well as satirical poetry: for the exercise of which talent he was refused his degree and expelled the University of Oxford. Aubrey frequently alludes to him as "The Serjeant;" and as all the Serjeant's manuscripts came at his death to his grandson, Sir John Hoskins, Aubrey's intimate friend, Aubrey would have the best authority for his statement. For a memoir of the Serjeant see Chalmers's Biog. Dict.

[2] "In Hammond Alley, Bishopsgate street, the farthest house." MS.

[3] He left no Will: and in the Letters of Administration taken out by his brother William he is described as "Bachelor."

John Britton F.S.A.

This name, familiar for half a century to the architects and artists of Great Britain, at length occupies its place in the Obituary of meritorious men. His life supplies one instance more of perseverance against difficulty, crowned with success. Not that his incessant labour led to much ultimate result as to any accumulation of worldly means: for at that *desideratum* he failed to arrive. He failed, because he was no selfish saver or worshipper of money for its own sake. It was in his sight a thing to be used: and the use to which he applied it was that of improving, in his own department, the taste of the age in which he lived. In this respect he was eminently successful: for by long-continued liberal efforts made with that object in view, he has secured for himself a name of authority in the remembrance of his country.

Of his early life, his struggles with adversity, and his many literary works, an authentic account may be found in his "Autobiography," the employment of his declining years, almost to the very day of death. Occasionally diffuse, it is upon the whole a curious and instructive memoir, showing (in his own words) "how much may be effected by zeal and industry, with moderate talents and without academic learning." Some things which as an autobiographer he could not, without breach of modesty, say of himself, may now be said of him by others. And it is the testimony of those who knew him well, that he had an active and penetrating mind, remarkable power of arrangement, an excellent memory, a kind heart, and a moral character free from reproach. He was simple in his habits, fond of children and a favourite with them; a great lover of Natural History, and an advocate of mercy to the humblest animal. In stature he was short; in figure slender: a ready and amusing speaker: of great vivacity and cheerfulness even to the last. Devoted to the Antiquities of his country, particularly his native county, he excelled in architectural illustration addressed to the eye. In this branch of Art, through tact in appreciating skill, he was the means of bringing into notice some of our best modern engravers.

John Britton's life commenced on the 7th July 1771; under

circumstances which without the aid of a Horoscope may safely be
pronounced to have been as unpromising as well could be. He was
born in a cottage (represented in the wood cut), still standing at

John Britton's Birth-place.

the angle formed by the main street of Kington St. Michael with
the lane that leads to the Church.[1] He was the fourth of ten
children, but eldest son, of Henry and Ann Britton, without inheritance or much prospect of it. His father's occupation included
various branches of petty village business. He was baker, maltster,
shopkeeper and small farmer: and a single room 14 feet wide by
$6\frac{1}{2}$ high, with a heavy beam across the ceiling and a floor of stone,
served for parlour, kitchen, hall, and nursery. Under-housed,
over-stocked with children, and encumbered with many trades
without success in any, the father sank into poverty. John received
instruction at a dame's school, and having mastered the "Chris-

---

[1] He was baptized August 4th by John Scrope, Vicar, (*Par. Reg.*) The
marriage of his parents Henry Britton and Ann Hillier, on 10th January 1765,
is registered at Norton about 5 miles from Kington St. Michael's. Her family
were at that time tenants of Maidford Farm in that parish: and in the first
cottage going from Maidford to Norton Church, Mr. Britton (as he told the
writer) learned his A B C.

cross Row" (like Aubrey, in the now rare horn-book), was removed for two years to a Mr. Moseley, a Baptist minister at Fosscote in Grittleton, thence to schools successively at Yatton Keynell, Draycote, and Chippenham. At thirteen he was taken away from education to carry loaves about on horseback to neighbouring villages. The mother was active and managing, and strove hard against misfortune: but bad debts, cheating millers, rivals in trade, and the heavy family, were too much for her, and she died broken-hearted. The father became idiotic; John's brothers and sisters were dispersed amongst relatives: and his own destiny was to be taken to London in October 1787, by an uncle Samuel Hillier, who after employing him for some time in his own house as a foot-boy with horses to clean, apprenticed him for six years to a Mr. Mendham of the Jerusalem Tavern, Clerkenwell. There, having paid no apprentice fee, he was not initiated into the deeper mysteries of the craft, but only into the duties of helper to a common porter, in bottling, corking, and binning wine.

The Jerusalem Tavern wine-cellar.

To his dismal life of ten hours a day in the Clerkenwell wine-vaults, with the choice, when his work was over, of either remaining in the cellar or associating with the workmen, Mr. Britton always looked back, as he well might, with utter abborrence. He learned nothing from the business, not even in what part of the world Oporto or Madeira were, lost his health, was afraid of complaining, and was only upheld through the period of legal imprisonment by the smiles of a young person in the establishment, with whom of course he fell in love. But even this cordial failing to restore him, his master at length gave up about half a year of his services, presented him with two guineas instead of twenty promised, and turned him out into the world to provide for himself. He had then two uncles in London, to whom he had been taught to look for friendly assistance. Both were living in genteel comfort, but at neither of their houses could he obtain even shelter from the weather, or a meal.

Before his first visit to London he had never seen a Dictionary, and knew nothing of geography or history : though as a boy he had been fond of books whenever he could get them. His self-education was continued underground and clandestinely. He would take an occasional half hour in the morning between seven and eight o'clock to look at the sky, breathe a little fresh air and visit two book stalls in the neighbourhood. His purchases were chiefly medical works, and those of Dr. Dodd, Ray, Smollett, Fielding and Sterne, &c. These he read by candle-light in the cellar at half hours abstracted from official duties, so that the tale of bottles to be corked had to be made up afterwards all the faster. One of the few acquaintances formed at this time was a Mr. Essex father of the present painter in enamel. From him books were borrowed, and at his house Britton first met his future friend and coadjutor in many literary undertakings, Mr. E. W. Brayley, then apprenticed as an enameller to Mr. Essex. In a memoir of his colleague published in the Gent. Mag. Dec. 1854, Mr. Britton says ; "From this unpromising association and from fortuitous circumstances, ultimately sprang a crop of literary works which cannot fail to astonish the reader who calculates their amount in volumes, pages, variety of subjects, extent of labour in research, travel, embellishment and manual writing." As may reasonably be supposed they commenced in the most humble departments of literature. The first partnership speculation was a song called "*The Powder Tax; or a Puff at the Guinea Pigs,*" written by Brayley and sung by Britton publicly at a club held at the Jacob's Well, Barbican, where a motley assemblage of smokers and tipplers met once a week to hear theatrical repetitions. The new ditty was encored, printed, and more than 70,000 copies sold by a song-dealer, who pirated this first publication of the two young authors.

The period between the release from the wine-cellar and the adoption of literature as a profession, embraced about seven years of privation and vicissitude, occasionally relieved by employment that produced a bare livelihood. In very poor and obscure lodgings at eightenpence a week he indulged in study, often reading in bed during the winter evenings to save the cost of firing. When the finances were in tolerable order he frequented "Free and easy," "Odd-fellows," and "Spouting clubs;" though never allowing his expenses to exceed sixpence a night at any of these choice associations. The next step was to Debating Societies, private theatricals and lectures, the last being rare.

But the first and all absorbing object after leaving Mr. Mendham's service was to undertake a journey on foot to Plympton in Devonshire, to renew with matrimonial intent the attachment formed for the goddess of the wine-cellar. Mr. Britton describes this toilsome journey and its result in a very amusing manner. The fair but faithless Dulcinea, some years older and apparently much wiser than himself, declined the suit, and he set off home again in a state of mental misery. At Bath he failed in obtaining an engagement as cellar-man at the White Hart Hotel, and returned to the metropolis shoeless, shirtless, and almost penniless. A short engagement at the London Tavern was followed by another as clerk to a widow in Smithfield; but the knavery and hypocrisy of the establishment disgusting him, he accepted a situation in the office of a Mr. Simpson, Attorney, in Gray's Inn, where he remained for three years at the wages of fifteen shillings a week. The business not being overwhelming gave him plenty of time for excursion in lighter walks, the drama, novels and poetry: and his income, small as it was, was sufficient to provide a decent lodging, clothes, food, and the luxury of books. For about ninepence a day during these three years, he dined at an eating-house in Great Turnstile, Holborn : where, amongst other characters, he met with the eccentric Sir John Dinely one of the poor Knights of Windsor, the noted Chevalier D'Eon, and Joseph Ritson the Antiquary.

His employer, the Gray's Inn Attorney, dying in 1798, a fresh engagement was made with Messrs. Parker and Wix, Solicitors, of Greville street, Hatton Garden, where he obtained twenty shillings a week, an augmentation of income peculiarly cheering, the new connexion being in other respects also very satisfactory. He now became member of a Debating Society in Coachmakers' Hall, and at the Shakesperian Theatre, Tottenham Court Road, not as a prominent orator, but as prompter and occasional helper in scenes. But at another club, the Jacob's Well, he rose to be a leading star by recitation of comic tales, prologues, and characters written by Peter Pindar, George Colman the younger, and others. These always amused and were often received with vociferous applause. Debating clubs at the close of the last century were a marked feature in London life; the excitement produced by the French Revolution was at its height, and the young men of the day hung upon the lips of the professors of democracy. Many of these were mere mob-orators, some were Government spies, some earnest politicians of ability; and of this class Mr. Britton has preserved some interesting reminiscences. In such a school no wonder that he contracted a propensity to express himself rather too strongly of those whose taste or views might not always be the same as his own : a habit that tinges now and then the writings even of his latest years. But

> "Quo semel est imbuta *recens*, servabit odorem
> Testa *diu*."[1]

His taste fixed on the drama, and in the winter of 1799 he was engaged by a Mr. Chapman at three guineas a week to write and sing at a theatre in Panton street, Haymarket, on the plan of the "Eidophusikon" of De Loutherbourg, a very popular entertainment

---

[1] Hor. E. I. 2. 69.   . . . . .   " A vessel, well
" With liquor seasoned, long retains the smell."

which under this difficult and therefore attractive name, exhibited exquisite scenery by that painter with the various effects of sunshine and gloom, morn, mid-day, night, thunder, lighting, &c.[1] Mr. Chapman's imitation presented less of the sublime and more of the miscellaneous; including, as it did, John Britton's monologue, the musical glasses, and a learned dog. This temple of the Muses being destroyed by fire in 1800, others were resorted to, and a large acquaintance was formed in histrionic society of every grade, from writers and actors down to mountebanks and clowns. Many are his anecdotes of these persons. Through the interest of the more distinguished actors, the Kembles, Bannister, Young, and others, he was supplied with orders for the theatre, and at that time believed it was impossible to be tired of reading plays or seeing them represented on the stage. The playhouse seemed the most fascinating place of rational amusement in the world, and he was on the eve of becoming an actor. The fascination fortunately passed away: the accounts of struggle and privation endured by friends who had embarked in that line damped his ambition, and he renounced the stage as a profession.

But for what was he fitted? Since emancipation from the Clerkenwell vaults his life had been one of uncertainty : and though fond of reading and eager for information, he had not dared to think of literature as a means of livelihood. Two or three juvenile essays slipped into the letter-box of a Shoe Lane periodical had indeed been printed, and their appearance in type was gratifying. He followed them up with comments on players, clubs and theatricals. For these a place was found in the "Sporting Magazine," published by John Wheble of Warwick Square, who proved a kind friend and was the cause of his becoming, ultimately and for life, an Author. A sixpenny pamphlet called "*The Thespian Olio,*" was the first book of which he was the Editor. Then followed a daring speculation (involving the risk of £15, a sum never hitherto in his possession at one time), the "*Odd Fellows' Song Book,*" price one shilling ! Of this 500 copies were printed and actually sold, bringing in a trifling profit. He then became connected with John

---

[1] See a description by W. H. Pyne in " Wine and Walnuts."

Fairburn a bookseller in the Minories, and wrote for him "*Twelfth Night Characters,*" to be printed on cards and drawn out of a bag, for the amusement of evening parties on that Festival. The hint was borrowed by others, and afterwards grew to an extensive trade. The next effort was in 1799, "*The Life and Adventures of Pizarro,*" a compilation that gave him his first taste of the difficulties of authorship, and for this, his maiden essay, he received ten pounds. Great was his self-satisfaction at beholding a superior edition, price five shillings!

But the turning point of his career had arrived: and a direction was now given to it from which he never afterwards swerved. As frequently happens, a trifling incident gave the bias. Amongst the articles contributed by him to the pages of Mr. Wheble's Sporting Magazine had been an anecdote of Britton's juvenile days, relating to a fox in his native village of Kington St. Michael. With 15 or 20 couple of the Duke of Beaufort's hounds almost at his brush, the animal had rushed into an open cottage at the foot of a hill in the village street, and jumping into a cradle where a

Little Red Riding Hood at Kington.

baby was asleep, crept under the clothes. The mother being in the garden and hearing the hounds in full cry towards her door, ran in to protect the child; its strange bedfellow was discovered and handed over to the less tender nursing of the huntsman.

The insertion of this Wiltshire anecdote in Mr. Wheble's periodical happened to turn the conversation upon that county, when the Editor told Britton that some years before, when living at Salisbury, he had conceived the idea of publishing a work in two volumes, to be called "The Beauties of Wiltshire," but had been prevented from continuing it. He now suggested the thought to the contributor of the fox story, urged him to undertake it, and offered pecuniary assistance. Being at the time without any sort of tie or profitable occupation, Britton caught eagerly at the suggestion; the more so as it would give him again and again the opportunity of revisiting and exploring his native county. Such was the *real* beginning of his literary life.

The task was accepted; without any previous qualifications whatever for performing it, other than those of ardour and perseverance. He knew nothing of the labour required for real topography, had never studied works upon the subject, and those he now looked into seemed dry and uninviting. Warner's "Walk through Wales" appeared to be more to the purpose, and taking this for his model he commenced a pedestrian tour. Armed with a few maps and books, a limited wardrobe and an umbrella, he rambled several hundred miles about the Midland Counties, passing through Wiltshire on his return. His whole expenses during several months amounted only to eleven pounds sixteen shillings and ninepence! Of this his first excursion Mr. Britton retained to the last a very vivid and minute recollection; and has devoted no less than 100 pages of his "Autobiography" to notices of the different places he visited, and the literary or otherwise eminent persons to whom he obtained introduction. One of these notices, presenting at the same time a fair sample of the general style of his book, will be more particularly acceptable to Wiltshire readers. It describes his reception at Bowood.[1]

"Up to the age of twenty-six, I had never conversed with a nobleman, or scarcely with a gentleman in the higher ranks of

---

[1] Autobiography, vol. i. p. 353.

society, and had never visited any of the wealthy mansions of the
great personages of the land.   I certainly had been admitted into
the studios of a few artists, and also into the wine-cellars of Sir
William Chambers, in Berners Street and at Whitton Park; and I
had spent two days with Mr. Scrope and his aged mother, at Castle
Combe, as will be noticed hereafter; but the last event occurred
immediately after my emancipation from the wine-cellar, and before
I undertook my Quixotic journey to Plympton, already noticed, or
had any notion of literature as a profession.   Otherwise my inter-
course with aristocracy and intellectual beings was as 'rare as snow
in June, or wheat in chaff.'   It is true that I was from boyhood
ambitious to be in the company of my elders and superiors in
knowledge; and a little of the rust and rudeness of village life and
menial manners had been rubbed down, if not polished, by partiality for debating societies and private theatricals, which were
popular in London at the beginning of the present century.   I
must frankly acknowledge that I was as unfitted for communion,
and unqualified to converse, with princes or nobles of the land, as
with utopian autocrats or celestial monarchs.   I approached the
house, through a lodge and park, which inspired awe and wonder;
I rang the bell to the domestic part of the premises with hesitation
and doubt; I asked incoherent questions about the Marquis, the
house, &c.; the porter was perplexed and called the footman, who
consulted the valet, and he appealed to the butler, who good-
naturedly construed my meaning and wishes, and introduced me
to his noble master, who was seated in a well-filled and spacious
library, and who appeared to my dizzy vision like something super-
human.   Without a card, or prospectus of the work which was the
ostensible object of my visit, I was requested to explain who I was,
and what was the nature of my inquiry and intentions.   Unpre-
pared to explain what I had no distinct notion of myself, I related
something of my short and uneventful career, and the reasons for
attempting to write about my native county; told of my friendless
and forlorn circumstances, love of reading, and the arts; desire to
acquire knowledge, and qualify myself to accomplish the task I had
undertaken with some degree of credit to myself, and not discredit

to my friends. From persons at Chippenham and from public report, I had been led to consider the Marquis as naturally high, stern, and haughty to strangers, and with this impression I approached him with a full recognition of the embarrassed situation of poor dear Goldsmith, in his interview with the Duke of Newcastle. Fortunately I found him very different from anticipation, for he was bland, courteous, and affable. Hence I was soon relieved from all painful restraint, and told my "round unvarnished tale" of birth-place near Bowood, of being parentless, friendless, and almost homeless, but ambitious to do something to mitigate those misfortunes.—After I had been indulged and honoured with nearly an hour's most exciting converse, his lordship called his librarian, Mr. Matthews, directed him to provide me with such books and maps as might be useful, allot me a bedroom, and send a person to show me the house, the pleasure-grounds, the cascade, the park, and other objects. Relieved from the painful suspense of doubt, anxiety, and alarm, my heart expanded, my mind was exhilarated, and every thing, scene, and person, seemed super-naturally exquisite and charmed. Had his lordship repulsed my first overtures, and sent me from his house with cold pride or indifference, it is probable that 'The Beauties of Wiltshire' would never have appeared before the public, nor its author ever have become known in the annals of literature. To Lord Lansdowne, therefore, am I indebted for the condescension and kindness he manifested towards an unknown and very humble person; who has laboured hard from that time to the present in the fields of literature and art to produce a succession and amount of books, which may be considered to equal, if not surpass, those of any other English author, in quantity and quality of embellishment, typography, and in varied matter and manner of their miscellaneous contents."

Half a guinea a week was his allowance from Wheble for writing the "*Beauties of Wiltshire.*" It appeared in two volumes in 1801. After all it contained only an account of a few places, chiefly in the south of the county, and was not a book likely to bring any reputation to its author. Of this no one was better aware than the author himself in after life; but the circumstances under which it was composed are sufficient apology for its deficiencies. A third volume relating to North Wilts, and far superior to the former, appeared after the more mellowed experience of twenty-four years.

In 1800 he had made another walking Tour in company with his friend Brayley, preliminary to a larger work for which they had jointly engaged, "*The Beauties of England and Wales.*" Between the 8th June and 20th September they travelled 1350 miles. So little were they aware of the nature of their undertaking, that this work was at first announced to be completed in six volumes within three years. Eventually it grew to twenty-six; but only the first eight were written by the original authors. "The history of this once popular publication" (says Mr. Britton), "in progress for nearly twenty years, would involve a curious and rather lamentable exposition of the "Quarrels of Authors" and their dissensions with publishers, as well as certain caprices and forbearances of the latter. My own personal share and miseries in this drama were often painful, always perplexing and oppressive. At length the authors separated, and engaged with the booksellers to be responsible for the writing of certain counties and volumes." Mr. Britton wrote Lancashire, Leicestershire, and Lincolnshire for the ninth volume: Monmouth, Norfolk, Northamptonshire, and Wiltshire.

In 1805 he showed Josiah Taylor, the architectural bookseller, some drawings of ancient buildings which the conductors of the "*Beauties of England*" had not thought calculated for its pages. After some consultation it was agreed to commence a new quarto work entitled the "*Architectural Antiquities of Great Britain.*" A plan was digested, a prospectus written, Longman and Co. engaging to take a third share and be the publishers. It extended to five quarto volumes, and brought before the public 365 engravings representing a great variety of old buildings, as well as many historical and descriptive essays by several pens. This work gave rise to a new school of artists, both draftsmen and engravers, as well as to many rival publications. It appeared in numbers, Mr. Britton receiving £30 per number for the first four volumes, with £10 additional for such numbers as were reprinted to meet an increased demand. The fifth

N

volume requiring much greater research, his remuneration was increased to £50 a number: and the total so charged by him amounted to more than £1800 during a period of 21 years. The sale of the four volumes was profitable throughout. The fifth, the most elaborate, barely paid its own expenses. The final balance-sheet after sale of stock, copper-plates, &c., showed a net general profit of about £9800 (from 1805 to 1826), the author's share of which was about £3266.[1]

In 1814 he commenced his magnificent work the "*Cathedral Antiquities of England,*" the Cathedral of his native county being the first. The whole was finished in 1835, containing in fourteen volumes, folio and quarto, with 311 engravings, an elaborate illustration of these noble English Edifices. The author was allowed £50 a number, but the work proving unprofitable, he reduced it to £30.[2] The production of these truly valuable volumes was carried on throughout under his immediate superintendence, many of the artists working in his own house and being trained to their task by himself. No one who has not been practically concerned in the preparation of an illustrated book for the press, can form any just idea of the immense amount, not only of capital, but of time, labour and mental anxiety which these must have required.

He continued the course of persevering and laborious authorship now specially his own,—that of architectural and topographical description and antiquities. To dwell on these in detail would occupy too much space. A list of his works is therefore appended, taken from the second volume of his "Autobiography."[3]   His

---

[1] A fine large paper copy of the "*Architectural Antiquities*" with choice proof impressions of the plates, *and the whole of the original drawings*, making eight volumes, was prepared for the late John Broadley, Esq., who paid Mr. Britton £500 for the set. This copy was subsequently bought at an auction by the late Joseph Neeld, Esq., and is now in the Library at Grittleton House.

[2] On many costly publications in which he was concerned, considerable loss was sustained. Of such works the purchasers are comparatively few, whilst the expenses are enormous. The Drawings supplied for the "*Cathedral Antiquities*" cost on an average about seven guineas each: whilst to the engraver, Mr. Le Keux, was frequently paid thirty to forty pounds for a single plate: in one instance (Bishop Bronscombe's monument in Exeter Cathedral) £52 10s.

[3] The greater part of this volume was prepared by his friend and assistant, Mr. T. E. Jones.

enterprising and active mind was incessantly at work, either in fulfilling old engagements or projecting new ones; in collecting materials for histories never to be completed, editing the compositions of others, contributing to periodicals, sorting, indexing, and arranging the contents of his own drawers and portfolios, and not least of all, in a very large correspondence. Besides all this, he acted for many years as Registrar of the "*Royal Literary Fund,*" and Honorary Secretary to the "*Wiltshire Society*" a charitable Institution founded in 1817. To the *Russell Institution*, the *Graphic Society*, the *Architects' and Antiquaries' Club*, and other associations of similar kind he gave much of his attention; and was one of the founders of the *Geographical Society*. In Wiltshire he was well known as a chief promoter of its first Topographical Society, and as a constant attendant upon the meetings of the one which exists at present.

It will be doing no injustice to the worth of this most indefatigable gentleman, to repeat now that he is no more, an opinion of his literary ability pronounced during his life. He was not a man of marked originality or great mental power; but as a careful and diligent writer in a branch of Literature insufficiently treated before his time, he did excellent service in calling the attention of the educated public to our long-neglected National Antiquities: and there can be little doubt that his elegantly illustrated works were a chief exciting cause in bringing about an improved state of public feeling towards those subjects.[1] And when the reader glances

---

[1] The English Encyclopædia. C. Knight, Art. Britton. The true point of Mr. Britton's merit is justly seized in the following passage of an address by Digby Wyatt, Esq., delivered at a general meeting of the Royal Institution of British Architects. "The pictorial illustrations of our national monuments at the close of the last century were of the most loose and imperfect description. Since the careful prints of Hollar, scarcely any engravings of architectural subjects had appeared worthy of notice or reliance; and the early productions of the Antiquarian Society presented the only approximation to accuracy. James Basire, Rooker, and Lowry, were the fashionable engravers of such subjects, and John Carter, and Fowler, who illustrated stained glass and ancient mosaics, almost the only trustworthy draughtsmen. It was mainly through Britton's energy that a reformation was effected. His activity and enthusiasm soon gathered about him all those rising men whose names are now so familiar to us. He saw from the improvements which had been effected, mainly by Stothard, and

once more at our woodcut of the miserable hovel in which John
Britton was born and reared, and recollects the obstacles in the
face of which he toiled from youth to age, relying on his own
energy and industry in struggles with the world; he will take up
the volumes of the "Autobiography" with an increased respect:
and will lay them down concurring in the remark made by Southey
on the very case; "Details of this kind carry with them an interest
to which no fiction can attain, and the memoirs of a man who,
from such circumstances and under such difficulties, made his way
to a station of respectability, is one of the most useful and encou-
raging lessons that can be placed in the hands of the young."

The origin of the two volumes of which the "Autobiography"
consists was this. On the 74th anniversary of his birthday a
number of his friends invited him to a dinner at the Castle Hotel,
Richmond, when eighty-two gentlemen were present. It was
determined to mark their esteem for him by a permanent testimonial, and a "Britton Club" was formed to carry out the project.
The testimonial, at his own suggestion was eventually made to take
the form of an "Autobiography," which he was to prepare and print
with the fund, amounting to £1000. These marks of respect and
cordial reception testify the general esteem in which he was held,
and his power of making and retaining friends; contrasting

Heath, the engraver, the capabilities of copper plate engraving; and speedily
brought to bear upon the long neglected antiquities of the country, that artistic
ability through the exercise of which they could alone be popularised. Samuel
Prout, Frederick Mackenzie, Edward Blore, George Cattermole, W. H. Bartlett,
R. W. Billings, Henry Shaw, and many more, were at various periods induced
to bestow their earnest efforts upon the proper delineation of those views which
were so successfully transferred to copper by the brothers, John and Henry Le
Keux, and other engravers, for the most part pupils of Basire. Public attention
was captivated by the excellencies of the engravings of the Architectural Antiquities of the land, and the excitement which at first took the form of vague
admiration, has in our time reached its happy consummation in profound inves-
tigation into the true principles upon which they depended for grandeur and
effect, and in a wise and wholesome spirit of conservancy. For much of this,
the country is deeply indebted to that friend we have so lately lost. His labours
were incessant, his memory extraordinary, his system admirable, his clearness
of understanding, and liveliness of fancy in no common wise vigorous, his
affections warm, his habits exemplary. Had he been less honest he might have
been far richer; had he been more selfish he would never have benefited his
country as he unquestionably did."

strangely with the coldness which he frequently complains of having met with when labouring to attract attention in earlier days.

He was twice married but had no family. His residence during the latter part of his life was in Burton street, Tavistock square. When Mr. Disraeli was Chancellor of the Exchequer his literary services were recognized by the grant of an annual pension of £75 : not excessive when compared with other bounties of the kind, but still an acceptable addition to the limited circumstances under which he closed his life. This he did, on Thursday the 1st January 1857, in his eighty-sixth year, and was buried at the Norwood Cemetery on the Thursday following : a Deputation from the Institute of British Architects, with many other friends, attending his remains to the grave.

By economy in other things he had formed a very extensive collection of books, prints, and other articles in the class of topographical literature. So inconveniently large at one time had this become that closets and shelves became crowded whilst his purse collapsed. In 1832 he disposed of a large quantity, sufficient to make a sixteen days sale. The rest have been sold by auction since his decease : that portion of them which related to his native county having been previously secured by the "Wiltshire Archæological Society.'   J. E. J.

A CLASSIFIED LIST

OF

THE LITERARY WORKS

OF

JOHN BRITTON, F.S.A.

With the Dates, the number of Pages and Prints: and the amount paid for Drawings, Engravings, Paper, Printing, &c.

CLASS I. WORKS BY J. BRITTON.

TITLE.	Vols.	Date.	Pages.	Engs.	Amt. pd. £.
1. The Beauties of Wiltshire	2	1801	668	15	—
2. Ditto. Vol. III. Also printed to form a separate Work, with title of "Topographical Sketches of North Wiltshire"	1	1825	440	16	500
3. The Architectural Antiquities Great Britain	4	1805 to 1818	450	279	13,088
4. Ditto. Vol. V. Also forming a separate Work, with the title of "A Chronological History of Christian Architecture in England," with copious Lists, Tables, Glossary, Indexes, &c.	1	1818 to 1826	324	86	4,004
5. Historical Account of Corsham House, Wilts	1	1806	108	1	70
6. The Pleasures of Human Life; or the "Miseries" turned Topsy-turvy	1	1807	239	8	90
7. Catalogue Raisonnée of the Cleveland Gallery	1	1808	158	2	150
8. Historical and Descriptive Account of Redcliffe Church, Bristol	1	1813	40	12	419
9. The Cathedral Antiquities of England	14	1814 to 1835	1388	311	19,008
10. The Rights of Literature, (pamphlet)	1	1814	77	—	30
11. Norwich Cathedral Vade-Mecum	1	1817	32	4	40
12. Historical and Descriptive Account of Fonthill Abbey, Wilts	1	1823	85	11	600

TITLE.	Vols.	Date.	Pages.	Engs.	Amt.pd. £.
13. Historical and Descriptive Account of Bath Abbey Church	1	1825	220	10	612
14. The Union of Architecture, Sculpture, and Painting, illustrated by a Description of the House, &c. of Sir John Soane...	1	1827	60	29	638
15. Specimens of the Architectural Antiquities of Normandy (Pugin and Le Keux)...	1	1828	40	80	1,700
16. A Brief Account of the Colosseum, London	1	1829	8	9	—
17. Picturesque Antiquities of English Cities..	1	1830	103	83	2,800
18. Descriptive Sketches of Tunbridge Wells..	1	1832	148	13	252
19. A Dictionary of the Architecture and Archæology of the Middle Ages		1832 to 1838	512	40	1,620
20. History, &c. of Cassiobury Park, Hertfordshire	1	1837	32	34	400
21. Account of the London and Birmingham Railway	1	1839	26	37	—
22. Account of Toddington, Gloucestershire ...	1	1840	70	31	400
23. Historical and Descriptive Notices of Windsor Castle..................	1	1842	12	42	—
24. Remarks and Suggestions on Redcliffe Church, Bristol, in an " Appeal to the Public, by the Churchwardens, &c."..	1	1842	26	5	—
25. An Essay on Topographical Literature, the National Records, &c., with Glossaries*	1	1843	66	—	—
26. Memoir of John Aubrey, F.R.S.*	1	1845	130	3	—

CLASS II. WORKS OF WHICH J. BRITTON AND
E. W. BRAYLEY WERE JOINT AUTHORS.

TITLE.	Vols.	Date.	Pages.	Engs.	Amt.pd. £.
27. The first eight Volumes of the Beauties of England and Wales. J. B. wrote the Accounts of the Counties of Lancaster, Leicester, and Lincoln, Vol. IX.—of those of Monmouth, Norfolk, Northampton, Vol. XI., and Wiltshire, Vol. XV.	11	1802 to 1814	7150	315	—
28. Memoirs of the Tower of London.........	1	1830	374	20	—
29. History of the Ancient Palace and Houses of Parliament, Westminster	1	1834 to 1836	476	48	—

* These works were published by the first Wiltshire Topographical Society.

TITLE.	Vols.	Date.	Pages.	Engs.	Amt.pd.£.

CLASS III. OF THESE WORKS J. BRITTON WAS EDITOR,
AND WROTE PORTIONS OF THE LITERARY MATTER.

TITLE.	Vols.	Date.	Pages.	Engs.	Amt.pd.£.
30. The Fine Arts of the English School	1	1812	126	24	3,144
31. The Public Buildings of London, from Drawings by A. Pugin...............	2	1825 to 1828	718	144	3,360

CLASS IV. J. BRITTON EDITED THE FOLLOWING, IN
THE OWNERSHIP OF WHICH HE WAS INTERESTED.

TITLE.	Vols.	Date.	Pages.	Engs.	Amt.pd.£.
32. Magazine of the Fine Arts	1	1821	480	6	200
33. Specimens of Gothic Architecture, engraved from Drawings by Augustus Pugin	2	1823 to 1825	144	114	2,872
34. Picturesque Views of English Cities, from Drawings by G. F. Robson	1	1828	16	32	2,010
35. A Narrative of Memorable Events in Paris, in 1815. Written by Mr. T. R. Underwood: edited and published by J. B. ..	1	1828	298	—	191
36. Anstey's "New Bath Guide," with Preface and Notes	1	1830	252	8	150
37. A Map of the Borough of Marylebone: two large sheets	1	1835	—	1	420
38. The West Fronts, Ground Plans, and Interiors of Fourteen English Cathedrals: two large plates, in aquatint ..	—	1829	—	2	60

CLASS V. J. BRITTON REVISED AND CORRECTED THE FOLLOWING WORKS,
BUT HAD NO SHARE IN THE OWNERSHIP.

TITLE.	Vol.	Date.
39. British Atlas. 58 Maps of the Counties of England and Wales, and 21 Plans of Cities and Towns.	1	1802 to 1817
40. The Picture of London	1	1832
41. Wild's Lincoln Cathedral	1	1837
42. Carter's Ancient Architecture	1	1837
43. Carter's Ancient Sculpture and Painting	1	1838
44. Brayley and Ferrey's Christ Church	1	1841
45. Aubrey's Natural History of Wiltshire*	1	1846

CLASS VI. THE FOLLOWING ARE CONTRIBUTIONS BY J. BRITTON TO
THE VARIOUS SERIAL WORKS REFERRED TO.

TITLE.	Vol.	Date.
46. The Articles relating to the Topography of England, Wales, and Scotland, in *Rees's Cyclopædia*	—	1802 to 1819

---

* Published by the first Wiltshire Topographical Society.

TITLE.	Vol.	Date
47. The Annual Review: the Notices of all Works on Topography..	7	1802 to 1808
48. Havell's Picturesque Views of Nobleman's and Gentleman's Seats, with descriptive Letter-press	1	1816 to 1824
49. Accounts of Bath and Bristol, for Jones's Illustrations of those Cities, from the Drawings of T. H. Shepherd...........	1	1829
50. Account of Edinburgh, for Jones's Illustrations of that City....	1	1830
51. Account of Cornwall, for Fisher's Illustrations of the County, from the Drawings of Allom, Bartlett, &c.	1	1832
52. The British Magazine: a Series of Articles, being "Historical Notices and Descriptions of Christian Architecture in England	—	1834
53. Fisher's Portrait Gallery; Memoirs of Sir John Soane, and of Sir Jeffrey Wyatville, to accompany their Portraits in this Work	—	1834
54. The Penny Cyclopædia: the articles Avebury and Stonehenge..	—	1835 1842

TOTALS FROM THE PRECEDING LIST: VIZ.—

57 *Volumes*, besides Essays.

Amount of *printed Pages* 17,254

Number of *Engravings* 1,867

Amount of *Monies expended* £50,328

** *In addition to the above the following* unpublished:—

Eight Lectures on the Architectural Antiquities of all Nations; illustrated by nearly 300 large Drawings. Read by the Author at the London Institution, &c.

A Lecture on Railways. Read at the Literary Institution, Bristol. 1833.

A Memoir of John Carter, Author of works on the Ancient Architecture, Sculpture, and Painting of England. Read at the Institute of British Architects. 1837.

Erratum. Page 57, line 24. For "deceased" *read* "ill-used."

H. BULL, Printer, Saint John Street, Devizes.

CPSIA information can be obtained at www.ICGtesting.com
Printed in the USA
LVOW01s0224070714

393076LV00020B/1279/P

9 781241 346164